QUESTIONS OF LIFE

To my wife, Pippa.

QUESTIONS OF LIFE

NICKY GUMBEL

Published in North America by Alpha North America, 2275 Half Day Road, Suite 185, Deerfield, IL 60015

This edition issued by special arrangement with Alpha International, Holy Trinity Brompton, Brompton Road, London SW7 1JA, UK

Questions of Life
by Nicky Gumbel

Originally published by KINGSWAY COMMUNICATIONS LTD, Lottbridge Drove, Eastbourne, BN23 6NT, England

First printed by Alpha North America in 2007

Printed in the United States of America

Illustrations by Charlie Mackesy

ISBN 978-1-934564-66-0

2 3 4 5 6 7 8 9 10 Printing/Year 14 13 12 11

CONTENTS

PREFACE

When *Questions of Life* was first published sixteen years ago, there were only a handful of Alpha courses running. As I write this, 14 million people have completed the course in 163 countries around the world.

Much of this is due to the extraordinary dedication, adaptability and hard work of Nicky Gumbel. But he would be the first to point out that there is another crucial factor: the Spirit of God seems to have adopted this course and has blown it along.

And this book, *Questions of Life,* has been central to the whole phenomenon. As the Alpha course in book form, it has become an international bestseller through which countless thousands have been introduced to Jesus Christ for the first time.

In it, Nicky provides some answers to the hunger and growing hope in every human heart that somewhere, somehow, there may be found a contemporary answer to the timeless question, "What is truth and how and where can we discover it?"

Questions of Life remains a sympathetic, fascinating, and immensely readable introduction to Jesus Christ—still the most attractive and captivating person it is possible to know. Nicky Gumbel's intelligent, well researched, and informed approach ensures that the search for Truth fully engages our minds as well as our hearts.

I have no hesitation in continuing to recommend this readable and important book.

Sandy Millar

FOREWORD

There is today a new interest in the Christian faith, and more specifically in the person of Jesus. Nearly two thousand years since His birth, He has approaching two billion followers. Christians will always be fascinated by the founder of their faith and the Lord of their lives. But now, there is a resurgence of interest among nonchurchgoers.

Many are asking questions about Jesus. Was He merely a man, or is He the Son of God? If He is, what are the implications for our everyday lives?

This book attempts to answer some of the key questions at the heart of the Christian faith. It is based on the Alpha course, which is designed for nonchurchgoers, those seeking to find out more about Christianity, and those who have recently come to faith in Jesus Christ. We have watched in astonishment as Alpha has spread to over 40,000 courses around the world. Millions of men and women of all ages have come on the course full of questions about Christianity, and have found God as their Father, Jesus Christ as their Savior and Lord, and the Holy Spirit as the One who comes to live within them.

I would like to thank all the people who have read and offered constructive criticisms on the manuscripts, and Cressida Inglis-Jones who typed the original manuscript and almost all the revisions with great speed, efficiency, and patience.

Nicky Gumbel

CHAPTER 1

IS THERE MORE TO LIFE THAN THIS?

For many years I had three objections to the Christian faith. First, I thought it was boring. I went to chapel at school and found it very dull. I had sympathy with the novelist Robert Louis Stevenson, who once entered in his diary, as if recording an extraordinary phenomenon, "I have been to church today, and am not depressed." My impression of the Christian faith was that it was dreary and uninspiring.

Secondly, it seemed to me to be untrue. I had intellectual objections to the Christian faith and described myself as an atheist. In fact, I rather pretentiously called myself a logical determinist. When I was fourteen I wrote an essay for religious studies in which I tried to destroy the whole of Christianity and disprove the existence of God. Rather surprisingly, it was nominated for a prize! I had knock-down arguments against the Christian faith and rather enjoyed arguing with Christians, on each occasion thinking I had won some great victory.

Thirdly, I thought that Christianity was irrelevant to my life. I could not see how something that happened 2,000 years ago and 2,000 miles away in the Middle East could have any relevance to my life today. At school we often used to sing that much-loved hymn "Jerusalem," which asks, "And did those feet in ancient time walk upon England's mountains green?" We all knew that the answer was, "No, they did not." Jesus never came anywhere near England!

With hindsight, I realize that it was partly my fault as I never really listened and so did not know very much about the Christian faith. There are many people today who don't know much about Jesus Christ, or what He did, or anything else about Christianity.

One hospital chaplain listed some of the replies he was given to the question, "Would you like Holy Communion?" These are some of the answers:

"No thanks, I'm Church of England."

"No thanks, I asked for Cornflakes."

"No thanks, I've never been circumcised."[1]

Not only was I ignorant about the Christian faith but, looking back, my experience was that something was missing.

In his book *The Audacity of Hope*, President Barack Obama, commenting on his own conversion to Christianity, writes of the hunger in every human heart:

> Each day, it seems, thousands of Americans are going about their daily rounds—dropping off the kids at school, driving to the office, flying to a business meeting, shopping at the mall, trying to stay on their diets—and coming to the realization that something is missing. They are deciding that their work, their possessions, their diversions, their sheer busyness are not enough. They want a sense of purpose, a narrative arc to their lives, something that will relieve a chronic loneliness or lift them above the exhausting, relentless toll of daily life. They need an assurance that

> somebody out there cares about them, is listening to them—that they are not just destined to travel down a long highway toward nothingness.[2]

Men and women were created to live in a relationship with God. Without that relationship there will always be a hunger; an emptiness, a feeling that something is missing. Bernard Levin, perhaps the greatest columnist of his generation, once wrote an article called "Life's Great Riddle, and No Time to Find its Meaning." In it he said that in spite of his great success he feared he might have "wasted reality in the chase of a dream."

> To put it bluntly, have I time to discover why I was born before I die? . . . I have not managed to answer the question yet, and however many years I have before me they are certainly not as many as there are behind. There is an obvious danger in leaving it too late . . . why do I have to know why I was born? Because, of course, I am unable to believe that it was an accident; and if it wasn't one, it must have a meaning.[3]

He was not religious, writing on one occasion, "For the fourteen thousandth time, I am not a Christian." Yet he seemed only too aware of the inadequate answers to the meaning of life. He wrote some years earlier:

> Countries like ours are full of people who have all the material comforts they desire, together with such non-material blessings as a happy family, and yet lead lives of quiet, and at times noisy, desperation, understanding nothing but the fact that there is a hole inside them and that however much food and drink they pour into it, however many motor cars and television sets they stuff it with, however many well balanced children and loyal friends they parade around the edges of it . . . it aches.[4]

Jesus Christ said, "I am the way and the truth and the life" (John 14:6). The implications of His claim were as startling in the first century as they are in the twenty-first. So what are we to make of it?

Direction for a lost world

First, Jesus said, "I am the way." When their children were younger, some friends of mine had a Swedish nanny. She was struggling to learn the English language, and still hadn't quite mastered all the English idioms. On one occasion, an argument broke out between the children in their bedroom. The nanny rushed upstairs to sort it out, and what she meant to say was, "What on earth are you doing?" What she actually said was, "What are you doing on earth?" This is a very good question, "What are we doing on earth?"

Leo Tolstoy, author of *War and Peace* and *Anna Karenina*, wrote a book called *A Confession* in 1879, in which he tells the story of his search for meaning and purpose in life. He had rejected Christianity as a child. When he left university he sought to get as much pleasure out of life as he could. He threw himself into the social worlds of Moscow and St. Petersburg drinking heavily, sleeping around, gambling, and leading a wild life. But he found it did not satisfy him.

Then he became ambitious for money. He had inherited an estate and made a large amount of money on his books. Yet that did not satisfy him either. He sought success, fame, and importance. These he also achieved. He wrote what the *Encyclopaedia Britannica* describes as "one of the two or three greatest novels in world literature." But he was left asking the question, "Well fine . . . so what?" to which he had no answer.

Then he became ambitious for his family—to give them the best possible life. He married in 1862 and had a kind, loving wife and thirteen children (which, he said, distracted him from any search for the overall meaning of life!). He had achieved all his ambitions and was surrounded by what appeared to be complete happiness. And yet one question brought him to the verge of suicide: "Is there any meaning in my life which will not be annihilated by the inevitability of death which awaits me?"

He searched for the answer in every field of science and philosophy. The only answer he could find to the question "Why do I live?" was that "in the infinity of space and the infinity of time infinitely small particles mutate with infinite complexity." Not finding that answer hugely satisfying, he looked round at his contemporaries and found that many of them were simply avoiding the issue. Eventually he found among

Russia's peasants the answer he had been looking for: their faith in Jesus Christ. He wrote after his conversion that he was "led inescapably by experience to the conviction that only . . . faith give[s] life a meaning."[5]

Over one hundred years later, nothing has changed. Freddie Mercury, the lead singer of the rock group Queen, who died at the end of 1991, wrote in one of his last songs on *The Miracle* album, "Does anybody know what we are living for?" In spite of the fact that he had amassed a huge fortune and had attracted thousands of fans, he admitted in an interview shortly before his death that he was desperately lonely. He said, "You can have everything in the world and still be the loneliest man, and that is the most bitter type of loneliness. Success has brought me world idolization and millions of pounds, but it's prevented me from having the one thing we all need—a loving, ongoing relationship."

Freddie Mercury was right to speak of an "ongoing relationship" as the one thing we all need. Ultimately there is only one relationship that is completely loving and totally ongoing: a relationship with God. Jesus said, "I am the way." He is the only One who can bring us into that relationship with God that goes on into eternity.

When I was a child our family had an old black and white television set. We could never get a very good picture: on one occasion, during the World Cup final in 1966, just as England was about to score a goal, the screen went fuzzy, disintegrating into lines. We were quite happy with it since we did not know anything different. We tried to improve the picture by walking on certain floorboards and standing in certain places near it. Then we discovered that what the television needed was an outside antenna! Suddenly we could get clear and distinct pictures. Our enjoyment was transformed. Life without a relationship with Jesus Christ is like the television without the antenna. Some people seem quite happy, because they don't realize that there is something better. Once we have experienced a relationship with God, the purpose and meaning of life become clearer. We see things that we have never seen and we understand why we were made.

Reality in a confused world

Secondly, Jesus said, "I am the truth." Sometimes people say, "It does not matter what you believe so long as you are sincere." But it is possible to be sincerely wrong. Adolf Hitler was sincerely wrong. His beliefs destroyed the lives of millions of people. The Yorkshire Ripper believed that he was doing God's will when he killed prostitutes. He too was sincerely wrong. His beliefs affected his behavior. These are extreme examples, but they make the point that it matters a great deal what we believe, because what we believe will dictate how we live.

Other people's response to a Christian may be, "It's great for you, but it is not for me." This is not a logical position. If Christianity is true, it is of vital importance to every one of us. If it is not true, it is not "great for us"—it is very sad, and it means that Christians are deluded. As the writer and scholar C. S. Lewis put it, "Christianity is a statement which, if false, is of no importance, and, if true, of infinite importance. The one thing it cannot be is moderately important."[6]

Is it true? Is there any evidence to support Jesus' claim to be "the truth"? These are some of the questions we will be looking at later in the book. The linchpin of Christianity is the resurrection of Jesus Christ from the dead and for that there is ample evidence, which we will look at in the following chapter.

I don't think I ever realized how much the course of history has been shaped by people who believed that Jesus really is "the truth." Lord Denning, widely thought of as one of the greatest legal minds in the twentieth century, was for nearly forty years President of the Lawyers' Christian Fellowship. He had applied his legendary powers of analysis to the historical evidence for Jesus' birth, death, and resurrection and concluded that Christianity was true.

I had not appreciated either that some of the most sophisticated philosophers the West has ever produced—Aquinas, Descartes, Locke, Pascal, Leibniz, Kant—were all committed Christians. In fact, two of the most influential philosophers living today, Charles Taylor and Alasdair MacIntyre, have both built a great deal of their work on a deep commitment to Jesus Christ.

Nor had I realized how many of the pioneers of modern science were Christian believers: Galileo, Copernicus, Kepler, Newton, Mendel, Pasteur, and Maxwell. This is still true of leading scientists today. Francis Collins, director of the Human Genome Project and one of the most respected geneticists in the world, tells of a mountain walk during which he was so overwhelmed by the beauty of creation that, in his words, "I knelt in the dewy grass as the sun rose and surrendered to Jesus Christ."[7]

These words highlight the fact that when Jesus said, "I am the truth," He meant more than just intellectual truth. He means a personal knowledge of someone who fully embodies that truth. The Hebrew understanding of truth is one of experienced reality. It's the difference between knowing something in your head and knowing it in your heart.

Suppose that before I met my wife Pippa I had read a book about her. Then, after I had finished reading the book I thought, "She sounds like an amazing woman. This is the person I want to marry." There would be a big difference in my state of mind then—intellectually convinced that she was a wonderful person—and my state of mind now after the experience of many years of marriage from which I can say, "I know she is a wonderful person." When a Christian says, in relation to his faith, "I know Jesus is the truth," he does not mean only that he knows intellectually that He is the truth, but that he has experienced Jesus as the truth.

Life in a dark world

Thirdly, Jesus said, "I am the life." The Christian view has always been that people are made in the image of God. As a result there is something noble about every human being. This conviction has been the driving force behind many of the great social reformers, from William Wilberforce to Martin Luther King, Jr. and Desmond Tutu. But there is also another side to the coin.

Alexander Solzhenitsyn, a Russian writer who won the Nobel Prize for Literature, converted to Christianity when in exile from the Soviet Union, said, "The line separating good and evil passes, not through

states, nor through classes, nor between political parties . . . but right through every human heart and through all human hearts."[8]

I used to think I was a "nice" person—because I didn't rob banks or commit other serious crimes. Only when I began to see my life alongside the life of Jesus Christ did I realize how much was wrong.

We all need forgiveness and it can only be found in Christ. Marghanita Laski, a humanist, made an amazing confession during a TV debate with a Christian. She said, "What I envy about you Christians is your forgiveness." Then she added rather wistfully, "I have no one to forgive me."[9]

What Jesus did when He was crucified for us was to pay the penalty for all the things that we have done wrong. We will look at this subject in more detail in chapter 3. We will see that He died to remove our guilt and to set us free from addictions, fear, and death.

Jesus not only died for us, He was also raised from the dead for us. In this act He defeated death. Jesus came to bring us "eternal life." Eternal life is a quality of life which comes from living in a relationship with God (John 17:3). Jesus never promised anyone an easy life, but He promised fullness of life (John 10:10).

Alice Cooper, the veteran rock musician, once gave an interview to *The Sunday Times* headlined: "Alice Cooper has a dark secret—the 53-year-old rocker is a Christian." In this interview, he describes his conversion to Christianity. "It hasn't been easy combining religion and rock. It's the most rebellious thing I've ever done. Drinking beer is easy. Trashing your hotel room is easy. But being a Christian, that's a tough call. That's real rebellion."[10]

The theologian and philosopher Paul Tillich described the human condition as one that always involves three fears: fear of guilt, fear of meaninglessness, and fear of death. Jesus Christ meets each of these fears head on, because He is "the way and the truth and the life."[11]

CHAPTER 2

WHO IS JESUS?

For much of my life I was not interested in Christianity. My father was a secular Jew and my mother rarely went to church. I was at times an atheist and at times an agnostic, unsure of what I believed. I had studied the Bible in religion classes at school, but had ended up rejecting it all and arguing against the Christian faith. On Valentine's night 1974, my convictions were challenged by my closest friend Nicky Lee. I had just returned from a party when Nicky and his girlfriend appeared and told me that they had just become Christians. I was horrified! I had come across Christians during the year that I had taken off between high school and university and I was deeply suspicious of them, in particular their tendency to smile so much.

I knew I had to help my friends, so I thought that I would embark on some thorough research of the subject. I happened to have a rather dusty copy of the Bible on my shelves, so that night I picked it up and started reading. I read all the way through Matthew, Mark, and Luke and halfway through John's Gospel. I fell asleep. When I woke up, I finished John's Gospel and carried on through Acts, Romans, and 1 and 2 Corinthians. I was completely gripped by what I read. Previously it had meant virtually nothing to me. This time it came alive and I could not put it down. It had a ring of truth about it. I knew as I read it I had to respond because it spoke so powerfully to me. Very shortly afterwards I put my faith in Jesus Christ.

However, later I spent nearly ten years studying law and practicing as a barrister—so for me evidence is very important. I could not have taken a blind leap of faith, but was willing to take a step of faith based on good historical evidence. In this chapter I want to examine some of this historical evidence.

I am told that in an old communist Russian dictionary Jesus is described as "a mythical figure who never existed." No serious historian would maintain that position today. There is a great deal of evidence for Jesus' existence. This comes not only from the Gospels and other Christian writings, but also from other sources. For example, the Roman historians Tacitus and Suetonius both write about Him. The Jewish historian Josephus, born in A.D. 37, describes Jesus and His followers thus:

> Now there was about this time, Jesus, a wise man, if it be lawful to call him a man, for he was a doer of wonderful works—a teacher of such men as receive the truth with pleasure. He drew over to him both many of the Jews, and many of the Gentiles.[12]

So there is evidence outside the New Testament for the existence of Jesus. Furthermore, the evidence in the New Testament is very strong. Sometimes people say, "The New Testament was written a long time ago. How do we know that what they wrote down has not been changed over the years?" The answer is that we do know, very accurately, through the science of textual criticism, what the New Testament writers wrote. Essentially, the shorter the time span between the date the manuscript was written and the earliest available copy, the more texts we have, and the higher the quality of the existing texts, the less doubt there is about the original.

The late Professor F. F. Bruce (who was Rylands Professor of Biblical Criticism and Exegesis at the University of Manchester) shows in his book, *The New Testament Documents: Are They Reliable?* how wealthy the New Testament is in manuscript attestation by comparing its texts with other historical works.[13] The following table summarizes the facts and shows the extent of the evidence for the New Testament's authenticity.

Work	When Written	Earliest Copies	Time Span (yrs)	No. of copies
Herodotus	488–428 B.C.	A.D. 900	1,300	8
Thucydides	c. 460–400 B.C.	c.A.D. 900	1,300	8
Tacitus	A.D. 100	A.D. 1100	1,000	20
Caesar's *Gallic War*	58–50 B.C.	A.D. 900	950	9–10
Livy's *History of Rome*	59 B.C.–A.D. 17	A.D. 900	900	20
New Testament	A.D. 40–100	A.D. 130 (full manuscripts A.D. 350)	300	5,000 + Greek 10,000 Latin 9,300 others

F. F. Bruce points out that for Caesar's *Gallic War* we have nine or ten copies and the oldest was written some 950 years later than Caesar's day. For Livy's *History of Rome* we have not more than twenty copies, the earliest of which comes from around A.D. 900, though none of these are complete. Of the fourteen books of Tacitus' *Histories* only twenty copies survive; of the surviving sixteen books of his *Annals*, ten portions of his two great historical works depend entirely on two manuscripts, one of the ninth century and one of the eleventh century. The history of Thucydides is known almost entirely from eight manuscripts belonging to c. A.D. 900. The same is true of Herodotus' *Histories*. Yet no classical scholar doubts the authenticity of these works, in spite of the large time gap and the relatively small number of manuscripts.

With regard to the New Testament, we have a great abundance of material. The New Testament was probably written between A.D. 40 and A.D. 100. We have excellent full manuscripts for the whole New Testament dating from as early as A.D. 350 (a time span of only 300 years), papyri containing most of the New Testament writings dating from the third century and even a fragment of John's Gospel which scientists have carbon-dated to around A.D. 125. There are over 5,000 Greek manuscripts, over 10,000 Latin manuscripts and 9,300 other manuscripts, together with more than 36,000 citings in the writings of the early church fathers. As one of the greatest ever textual critics, F. J. A. Hort, said, "In the variety and fullness of the evidence on which it rests, the text of the New Testament stands absolutely and unapproachably alone among ancient prose writings."[14]

F. F. Bruce summarizes the evidence by quoting Sir Frederic Kenyon, a leading scholar in this area:

> The interval then between the dates of original composition and the earliest extant evidence becomes so small as to be in fact negligible, and the last foundation for any doubt that the Scriptures have come down to us substantially as they were written has now been removed. Both the *authenticity* and the *general integrity* of the books of the New Testament may be regarded as finally established.[15]

We know then from different types of evidence both outside and inside the New Testament that Jesus existed.[16] But who is He? I heard Martin Scorsese say on television that he made the film *The Last Temptation of Christ* in order to show that Jesus was a real human being. Yet that is not the issue at the moment. Few people today would doubt that Jesus was fully human. He had a human body; He was sometimes tired (John 4:6) and hungry (Matthew 4:2). He had human emotions; He was angry (Mark 11:15-17), He loved (Mark 10:21) and He was sad (John 11:35). He had human experiences; He grew up in a family (Mark 6:3), He had a job (Mark 6:3), He was tempted (Mark 1:13) and He experienced suffering and death (Mark 15:15-40).

What many say today is that Jesus was only a human being—albeit a great religious teacher. The comedian Billy Connolly spoke for many when he said, "I can't believe in Christianity, but I think Jesus was a wonderful man." What evidence is there to suggest that Jesus was more than just a man of staggering influence or a great moral teacher? The answer, as we shall see, is that there is a great deal of evidence. This evidence supports the Christian contention that Jesus was and is the unique Son of God, the second Person of the Trinity.

What did He say about Himself?

Some people say, "Jesus never claimed to be God." Indeed, it is true that Jesus did not go around saying the words, "I am God." Yet when one looks at all He taught and claimed, there is little doubt that He was conscious of being a person whose identity was God.

Teaching centered on Himself

One of the fascinating things about Jesus is that so much of His teaching was centered on Himself. Most religious leaders point away from themselves and to God, as we would expect. Jesus, the most humble and self-effacing Person who ever lived, in pointing people to God, pointed to Himself. He said, in effect, "If you want to have a relationship with God, you need to come to me" (John 14:6). It is through a relationship with Him that we encounter God.

There is a hunger deep within the human heart. Three leading psychologists of the twentieth century have all recognized this. Freud said, "People are hungry for love." Jung said, "People are hungry for security." Adler said, "People are hungry for significance." Jesus said, "I am the bread of life" (John 6:35). In other words, "If you want your hunger satisfied, come to me."

Addiction is a major problem in our society. Speaking about Himself, Jesus said, "If the Son sets you free, you will be free indeed" (John 8:36).

Many people are depressed, disillusioned, and in a dark place. Jesus said, "I am the light of the world. Whoever follows me will never walk in darkness, but will have the light of life" (John 8:12). For me, when I became a Christian, it was as if the light had suddenly been turned on and I could see things for the first time.

Many are fearful of death. One woman said to me that sometimes she couldn't sleep and that she would wake up in a cold sweat, frightened about death, because she didn't know what was going to happen when she died. Jesus said, "I am the resurrection and the life. He who believes in me will live, even though he dies; and whoever lives and believes in me will never die" (John 11:25-26). Mother Teresa was asked shortly before her death, "Are you afraid of dying?" She replied, "How can I be? Dying is going home to God. I've never been afraid. No. On the contrary, I'm really looking forward to it!"

Many people are burdened by worry, anxiety, fear, and guilt. Jesus said, "Come to me, all you who are weary and burdened, and I will give you rest" (Matthew 11:28). Many today are not sure how to live their lives, or whom they should follow. I can remember, before I was a Christian, that I would be impressed by someone and want to be like them, but before long it would be a different person, and then another. Jesus said, "Follow me" (Mark 1:17).

He said to receive Him was to receive God (Matthew 10:40), to welcome Him was to welcome God (Mark 9:37) and to have seen Him was to have seen God (John 14:9). A child once drew a picture and her mother asked what she was doing. The child said, "I am drawing a picture of God." The mother said, "Don't be silly. You can't draw a picture of God. No one knows what God looks like." The child replied, "Well, they will by the time I have finished!" Jesus said in effect, "If you want to know what God looks like, look at me."

Indirect claims

Jesus said a number of things which, although not direct claims to be God, show that He regarded Himself as being in the same position as God, as we will see in the examples which follow.

Jesus' claim to be able to forgive sins is well known. For example, on one occasion He said to a man who was paralyzed, "Son, your sins are forgiven" (Mark 2:5). The reaction of the religious leaders was, "Why does this man talk like that? He's blaspheming! Who can forgive sins but God alone?" Jesus went on to prove that He did have the authority to forgive sins by healing the paralyzed man. This claim to be able to forgive sins is indeed an astonishing claim.

C. S. Lewis puts it well in his book *Mere Christianity*:

> One part of the claim tends to slip past us unnoticed because we have heard it so often that we no longer see what it amounts to. I mean the claim to forgive sins: any sins. Now unless the speaker is God, this is really so preposterous as to be comic. We can all understand how a man forgives offenses against himself. You tread on my toes and I forgive you, you steal my money and I forgive you. But what should we make of a man, himself unrobbed and untrodden on, who announced that he forgave you for treading on other men's toes and stealing other men's money? Asinine fatuity is the kindest description we should give of his conduct. Yet this is what Jesus did. He told people that their sins were forgiven, and never waited to consult all the other people whom their sins had undoubtedly injured. He unhesitatingly behaved as if He was the party chiefly concerned, the person chiefly offended in all offenses. This makes sense only if He really was the God whose laws are broken and whose love is wounded in every sin. In the mouth of any speaker who is not God, these words would imply what I can only regard as a silliness and conceit unrivalled by any other character in history.[17]

Another extraordinary claim that Jesus made was that one day He would judge the world (Matthew 25:31-32). He said He would return and "sit on his throne in heavenly glory" (v. 31). All the nations would be gathered before Him. He would pass judgment on them. Some would receive eternal life and an inheritance prepared for them since the creation of the world, but others would suffer the punishment of being separated from Him forever.

Jesus said He would decide what happens to every one of us at the end of time. Not only would He be the Judge, He would also be the criterion of judgment. What happens to us on the Day of Judgment depends on how we respond to Jesus in this life (Matthew 25:40, 45).

Suppose you saw a man with a megaphone shouting, "On the Day of Judgment you will all appear before me and I will decide your eternal destiny. What happens to you will depend on how you've treated me and my followers." For a mere human being to make such a claim would be preposterous. Here we have another indirect claim to have the identity of Almighty God.

Direct claims

When Jesus was asked, "Are you the Christ, the Son of the Blessed One?" Jesus replied:

> "I am . . . and you will see the Son of Man sitting at the right hand of the Mighty One and coming on the clouds of heaven." The high priest tore his clothes. "Why do we need any more witnesses?" he asked. "You have heard the blasphemy. What do you think?" (Mark 14:61-64)

In this account it appears that Jesus was condemned to death for the assertion He made about Himself. A claim tantamount to a claim to be God was blasphemy in Jewish eyes, worthy of death.

On one occasion, when the Jews started to stone Jesus, He asked, "Why are you stoning me?" They replied that they were stoning Him for blasphemy "because you, a mere man, *claim to be God*" (John 10:33, italics mine). His enemies clearly thought that this was exactly what He was declaring.

When Thomas, one of His disciples, knelt down before Jesus and said, "My Lord and my God" (John 20:28), Jesus didn't turn to Him and say, "No, no, don't say that; I am not God." He said, "Because you have seen me, you have believed; blessed are those who have not seen and yet have believed" (John 20:29). He rebuked Thomas for being so slow to get the point!

If somebody makes claims like these they need to be tested. There are all sorts of people who make all kinds of claims. The mere fact that somebody claims to be someone does not mean that they are right. There are many people, some in psychiatric hospitals, who are deluded. They think they are Napoleon or the Pope, but they are not. So how can we test people's claims?

Jesus claimed to be the unique Son of God—God made flesh. There are three logical possibilities. If the claims were untrue, either He knew they were untrue—in which case He was an imposter, and an evil one at that. That is the first possibility. Or He did not know—in which case He was deluded; indeed, He was insane. That is the second possibility. The third possibility is that the claims were true.

C. S. Lewis pointed out that: "A man who was merely a man and said the sort of things Jesus said would not be a great moral teacher."

He would either be insane or else He would be "the devil of hell." "You must make your choice," he writes. Either Jesus was, and is, the Son of God or else He was insane or evil but, C. S. Lewis goes on, "let us not come up with any patronizing nonsense about His being a great human teacher. He has not left that open to us. He did not intend to."[18]

What evidence is there to support what He said?

In order to assess which of these three possibilities is right we need to examine the evidence we have about His life.

His teaching

The teaching of Jesus is widely acknowledged to be the greatest teaching that has ever fallen from human lips. The Sermon on the Mount contains some supremely challenging and radical teaching: "Love your enemies" (Matthew 5:44); "Turn the other cheek" (Matthew 5:39); "Do to others as you would have them do to you" (Luke 6:31).

John Mortimer, creator of the television series *Rumpole*, explained why, although a long-term atheist, he described himself as "a leading member of the Atheists for Christ Society"! When asked what brought about this change, he said, "Seeing the impact on society of a generation that has rejected God and, as a result, Christian ethics. What is beyond doubt is that the Gospels provide a system of ethics to which we must return if we are to avoid social disasters." The article, which appeared in *The Mail on Sunday* in April 1995, was headlined: "Even the Unbelievers Should Go back to Church Today."

Jesus' teaching is the foundation of our entire civilization in the West. Most of our laws were originally based on His teaching. We are making progress in virtually every field of science and technology. We travel faster and know more, and yet in the past 2,000 years no one has improved on the moral teaching of Jesus Christ.

Bernard Ramm, an American professor of theology, said this about the teachings of Jesus:

> They are read more, quoted more, loved more, believed more, and translated more because they are the greatest words ever spoken ...Their greatness lies in the pure lucid spirituality in dealing clearly, definitively, and authoritatively with the greatest problems that throb in

> the human breast . . . No other man's words have the appeal of Jesus' words because no other man can answer these fundamental human questions as Jesus answered them. They are the kind of words and the kind of answers we would expect God to give.[19]

His works

To test the extraordinary claims Jesus made, it makes sense to look not only at what He said but also at what He did. Jesus said that the miracles He performed were in themselves evidence that "the Father is in me, and I in the Father" (John 10:38).

Jesus must have been the most extraordinary person to have around. Sometimes people say that Christianity is boring. Well, it was not boring being with Jesus.

When He went to a party, He turned water into wine (John 2:1-11). He received one man's picnic and multiplied it so that it could feed thousands (Mark 6:30-44). He had control over the elements and could speak to the wind and the waves and thereby stop a storm (Mark 4:35-41). He carried out the most remarkable healings: opening blind eyes, causing the deaf and dumb to hear and speak, and enabling the paralyzed to walk again. When He visited a hospital a man who had been an invalid for thirty-eight years was able to pick up his bed and walk (John 5:1-9). He set people free from evil forces which had dominated their lives. On occasion, He even brought those who had died back to life (e.g., John 11:38-44).

Yet it was not just His miracles that made His work so impressive. It was His love, especially for the loveless (such as lepers and prostitutes), which seemed to motivate all that He did. The supreme demonstration of His love for us was shown on the cross when He laid down His life "for his friends" (John 15:13). Surely these are not the actions of an evil or deluded man?

His character

The character of Jesus has impressed millions who would not call themselves Christians. For example, Bernard Levin wrote of Jesus: "Is not the nature of Christ, in the words of the New Testament, enough to pierce to the soul anyone with a soul to be pierced? . . . he still looms over the world, his message still clear, his pity still infinite, his consolation still effective, his words still full of glory, wisdom and love."[20] Time magazine said this: "Jesus, the most persistent symbol of purity, selflessness and love in the history of Western humanity."

Here was someone who exemplified supreme unselfishness but never self-pity; humility but not weakness; joy but never at another's expense; kindness but not indulgence. He was a person in whom even His enemies could find no fault and whose friends said He was without sin. It has been said that our character is truly tested when we are under pressure or in pain. When Jesus was being tortured, He said, "Father, forgive them, for they do not know what they are doing" (Luke 23:34). Surely no one could suggest that such a man was evil or unbalanced?

His fulfillment of Old Testament prophecy

Jesus fulfilled over 300 prophecies (spoken by different voices over 500 years), including twenty-nine major prophecies fulfilled in a single day—the day He died. Although some of these prophecies may have found fulfillment at one level in the prophet's own day, they found their ultimate fulfillment in Jesus Christ.

I suppose it could be suggested that Jesus was a clever con man who deliberately set out to fulfill these prophecies in order to show that He was the Messiah foretold in the Old Testament.

The problem with that suggestion is, first, that the sheer number of them would have made it extremely difficult. Secondly, humanly speaking He had no control over many of the events. For example, the exact manner of His death was foretold in the Old Testament (Isaiah 53), the place of His burial and even the place of His birth (Micah 5:2). Suppose Jesus had been a con man wanting to fulfill all these prophecies. It would have been a bit late by the time He discovered the place in which He was supposed to have been born!

His resurrection

The physical resurrection from the dead of Jesus Christ is the cornerstone of Christianity. For me, it was through the life, death, and in particular the resurrection of Jesus that I came to believe that there is a God.

The Rev. Tom Wright, professor of New Testament and Early

Christianity at the University of St. Andrews, said this, "The Christian claim is not that Jesus is to be understood in terms of a God about whom we already know; it is this: the resurrection of Jesus strongly suggests that the world has a Creator, and that that Creator is to be seen in terms of, through the lens of, Jesus." But what is the evidence that the resurrection really happened? I want to summarize the evidence under four main headings.

1. His absence from the tomb. Many theories have been put forward to explain the fact that Jesus' body was absent from the tomb on the first Easter Day, but none of them is very convincing.

First, it has been suggested that Jesus did not die on the cross, but that He was still alive when He was put in the tomb and that He later recovered. But the physical trauma of a Roman flogging was enough to kill many people. This was graphically brought to life in Mel Gibson's film *The Passion of the Christ*. Jesus was then nailed to a cross and hung upright for six hours. Could a man in this condition push away a stone weighing probably a ton and a half? The soldiers were clearly convinced that He was dead or they would not have taken His body down from the cross. If they had allowed a prisoner to escape, they would have been liable to the death penalty. One New Testament scholar has joked that the only intriguing aspect of this theory is that it keeps coming back from the dead!

Furthermore, when the soldiers discovered that Jesus was already dead, "one of the soldiers pierced Jesus' side with a spear, bringing a sudden flow of blood and water" (John 19:34). This appears to be the separation of clot and serum which we know today is strong medical evidence that Jesus was dead.[21] John did not write it for that reason; he would not have possessed that knowledge, which makes it even more powerful evidence that Jesus was indeed dead.

Second, some have suggested that the disciples stole the body and began a rumor that Jesus had risen from the dead. Leaving aside the fact that the tomb was guarded, this theory is psychologically improbable. The disciples were depressed and disillusioned at the time of Jesus' death. It would have needed something extraordinary to transform the apostle Peter from a dejected and despondent deserter into the man who preached so powerfully at Pentecost that 3,000 people were converted.

In addition, when one considers how much they had to suffer for what they believed (floggings, torture, and for some even death), it seems inconceivable that they would be prepared to endure all that for something they knew to be untrue.

Third, some have said that the authorities stole the body. This seems the least probable theory of all. If the authorities had stolen the body, why did they not produce it when they were trying to quash the rumor that Jesus had risen from the dead? The authorities (both Jewish and Roman) would certainly have used all the many resources at their disposal to display Jesus' body publicly if they had actually been able to locate it.

Perhaps the most fascinating piece of evidence relating to Jesus' absence from the tomb is John's description of the grave-clothes. In a way, the "empty tomb" is a misnomer. When Peter and John went to the tomb they saw the grave-clothes which were, as the Christian author Josh McDowell puts it, "like the empty chrysalis of a caterpillar's cocoon"—when the butterfly has emerged.[22] It was as if Jesus had simply passed through the grave-clothes. Not surprisingly, John "saw and believed" (John 20:8).

2. *His appearances to the disciples.* Were these hallucinations? *The Concise Oxford Dictionary* describes a hallucination as an ". . . apparent perception of an external object not actually present." Hallucinations normally occur in highly strung, highly imaginative and very nervous people, or in people who are sick or on drugs. The disciples do not fit into any of these categories. Burly fishermen, tax collectors, and skeptics like Thomas are not likely candidates for mass hallucinations! Furthermore, people who hallucinate would be unlikely suddenly to stop doing so. Jesus appeared to His disciples on eleven different occasions over a period of six weeks. The number of occasions and the sudden cessation make the hallucination theory highly improbable.

Furthermore, over 500 people saw the risen Jesus. It is possible for one person to hallucinate. Maybe it is possible for two or three people to share the same hallucination. But is it likely that 500 people would all share the same hallucination? Finally, hallucinating is subjective. There is no objective reality—it is like seeing a ghost. Jesus could be touched, He ate a piece of grilled fish (Luke 24:42-43) and on one occasion He cooked breakfast for the disciples (John 21:1-14). Peter says, "[They] ate and drank with him after he rose from the dead" (Acts 10:41). He held long conversations with them, teaching them many things about the kingdom of God (Acts 1:3).

3. The immediate effect. The fact of Jesus rising from the dead, as one would expect, had a dramatic impact on the world. The church was born and grew at a tremendous rate. As Michael Green, writer of many popular and scholarly works puts it:

> [The] church . . . beginning from a handful of uneducated fishermen and tax gatherers, swept across the whole known world in the next three hundred years. It is a perfectly amazing story of peaceful revolution that has no parallel in the history of the world. It came about because Christians were able to say to inquirers: "Jesus did not only die for you. He is alive! You can meet him and discover for yourself the reality we are talking about!" They did, and joined the church, and the church, born from that Easter grave, spread everywhere.[23]

4. Christian experience. Countless millions of people down through the ages have experienced the risen Jesus Christ. They consist of people of every color, race, tribe, continent, and nationality. They come from different economic, social, and intellectual backgrounds.

Millions of Christians all over the world today are experiencing a relationship with the risen Jesus Christ. Over the years I have also experienced that Jesus Christ is alive today. I have experienced His love, His power, and the reality of a relationship that convinces me that He really is alive. As the fictional character Sherlock Holmes said, "When you have eliminated the impossible, whatever remains, however improbable, must be the truth."[24]

We saw, when we looked earlier in the chapter at what Jesus said about Himself, that there were only three realistic possibilities—either He was and is the Son of God, or else deluded or something more sinister. When one looks at the evidence it does not make sense to say that He was insane or evil. The whole weight of His teaching, His works, His character, His fulfillment of Old Testament prophecy, and His conquest of death make those suggestions absurd, illogical, and unbelievable. On the other hand, they lend the strongest possible support to Jesus' own self-understanding as a man whose identity was God.

In conclusion, as C. S. Lewis pointed out: "We are faced then with a frightening alternative." Either Jesus was (and is) exactly what He said, or else He was insane or something worse. To C. S. Lewis it seemed clear that He could have been neither insane nor evil, and thus he concludes, "However strange or terrifying or unlikely it may seem, I have to accept the view that He was and is God."[25]

CHAPTER 3

WHY DID JESUS DIE?

What do Madonna, Elton John, Bono, and the Pope have in common? One answer is that they all wear a cross. Many people today go around with a cross on their earrings, bracelet, or necklace or even etched on their body as a tattoo. We are so used to seeing this we are not shocked by it. But we might be shocked if we saw someone wearing a gallows or an electric chair round their neck, and the cross was just as much a form of execution. Indeed, it was one of the cruelest forms of execution known to humankind. It was abolished in A.D. 337 because ultimately even the Romans considered it too inhumane.

"umm.. They all have
"O" in their names?"

Yet the cross has always been regarded as the symbol of the Christian faith. A high proportion of the Gospels is about the death of Jesus. Much of the rest of the New Testament is concerned with explaining what happened on the cross—why Jesus died. The central service of the church, the Communion service, focuses on the broken body and shed blood of Jesus. Churches are often built in the shape of a cross. When the apostle Paul went to Corinth he said, "I resolved to know nothing while I was with you except Jesus Christ and him crucified" (1 Corinthians 2:2). Most leaders who have influenced nations or even changed the world are remembered for the impact of their lives. Jesus, who more than any other person changed the face of world history, is remembered for His death even more than for His life.

Why is there such concentration on the death of Jesus? What is the difference between His death and the death of Socrates or one of the martyrs or of a war hero? What did it achieve? What does it mean when the New Testament says He died "for our sins"? Why did He die for our sins? The answer in a nutshell is "because God loves you." Raniero Cantalamessa, Preacher to the Papal Household, said, "The love of God is the answer to all the 'whys' in the Bible: the why of creation, the why of the incarnation, the why of redemption."[26] It is because "God so loved the world" that He sent His one and only Son to die for us so that "whoever believes in him shall not perish but have eternal life" (John 3:16).

The problem

Sometimes people say, "I have no need for Christianity." They say something along the lines of, "I am quite happy, my life is full, and I try to be nice to other people and lead a good life." According to the Bible, every human being is created in the image of God. There is therefore something good and noble about every person. As I mentioned in chapter 1, this understanding of human nature has been a tremendous force for good in world history. In fact, it has laid the foundations for our modern understanding of human dignity and human rights by insisting that we are more than just bundles of genes and products of our environment. There is, however, a flip side to the coin. Certainly in my own life I would have to admit there are things I do that I know are wrong—I make mistakes. In order to understand why Jesus died we have to go back and look at the greatest problem that confronts every person.

If we are honest, we would all have to admit that we do things we know are wrong. Paul wrote: "All have sinned and fall short of the glory of God" (Romans 3:23). In other words, relative to God's standards we all fall a long way short. If we compare ourselves to armed robbers or child molesters or even our neighbors, we may think we come off quite well. But when we compare ourselves to Jesus Christ, we see how far short we fall. Somerset Maugham once said, "If I wrote down every thought I have ever thought and every deed I have ever done, men would call me a monster of depravity."[27]

The essence of sin is rebellion against God—our ignoring God in the sense of behaving as if He does not exist (Genesis 3), or choosing to do things that are wrong; with the result that we are cut off from Him. Like the Prodigal Son (Luke 15), we find ourselves far from our Father's home having made a mess of our lives. Sometimes people say, "If we are all in the same boat, does it really matter?" The answer is that it does matter because of the consequences of sin. These can be summarized under four headings.

The pollution of sin

Jesus said that it is possible for us to pollute the lives God has given us. Jesus said, "What comes out of you is what makes you 'unclean.' For from within, out of your hearts, come evil thoughts, sexual immorality, theft, murder, adultery, greed, malice, deceit, lewdness, envy, slander, arrogance and folly. All these evils come from inside and make you 'unclean'" (Mark 7:20-23). These things pollute our lives.

You may say, "I do not do most of these things." But one of them alone is enough to mess up our lives. We might wish the Ten Commandments were like an examination paper in which we only have to "attempt any three" of them. But the New Testament says that if we break any part of the Law we are guilty of breaking all of it (James 2:10). It is not possible, for example, to have a "reasonably clean" driving record. Either it is clean or it is not. One driving offense stops it from being a clean record. So it is with us; one offense makes our lives unclean.

The power of sin

The things we do wrong often have an addictive power. Jesus said, "Everyone who sins is a slave to sin" (John 8:34). It is easier to see this in some areas of our wrong-doing than in others. For example, it is well known that if someone takes a hard drug like heroin, it soon becomes an addiction.

It is also possible to be addicted to bad temper, envy, arrogance, pride, selfishness, slander, or sexual immorality. These things can take hold of our lives. We can become addicted to patterns of thought or behavior which, on our own, we cannot break. This is the slavery which Jesus spoke about. This is what has such a destructive power over our lives.

Bishop J. C. Ryle, a former bishop of Liverpool, once wrote:

> Each and all [sins] have crowds of unhappy prisoners bound hand and foot in their chains ... The wretched prisoners ... boast sometimes that they are eminently free ... There is no slavery like this. Sin is indeed the hardest of all task-masters. Misery and disappointment by the way, despair and hell in the end—these are the only wages that sin pays to its servants.[28]

The penalty for sin

There is something in human nature which cries out for justice. When we see children molested or old people attacked brutally in their homes, we long for the people who have done these things to be caught and punished. We believe there should be a penalty. Often our motives may be mixed: there may be an element of revenge as well as a desire for justice. But there is such a thing as justified anger. We are right to feel that sins should be punished and that people who do such things should not get away with them.

It is not just other people's sins that deserve punishment; it is our own as well. One day we will all be subject to the judgment of God. St. Paul tells us that "the wages of sin is death" (Romans 6:23).

The partition of sin

The death Paul speaks of is not only physical. It is a spiritual death, which results in eternal isolation from God. This cutting off from God begins now. The prophet Isaiah proclaimed, "Surely the arm of the Lord is not too short to save, nor his ear too dull to hear. But your iniquities have separated you from your God; your sins have hidden his face from you, so that he will not hear' (Isaiah 59:1-2). The things we do wrong cause this barrier. It is similar to when we have a falling out with someone and we cannot look them in the eye. There is something between us. Sometimes people say, "I've tried praying but my prayers seem to hit the ceiling." There is a partition: the things we do wrong have built a barrier between us and God.

The solution

We all need to deal with the problem of sin in our lives. The greater our understanding of our need the more we will appreciate what God has done. The good news of Christianity is that God loves us and He did not leave us in the mess that we make of our own lives.

In the person of His Son Jesus, God came to earth to die instead of us (2 Corinthians 5:21; Galatians 3:13). This has been called the "self-substitution of God."[29] In the words of the apostle Peter, "He himself bore *our* sins in *his* body on the tree . . . by *his* wounds you have been healed" (1 Peter 2:24, italics mine).

On the last day of July 1941 the sirens of Auschwitz announced the escape of a prisoner. As a reprisal, ten of his fellow prisoners would die—a long, slow starvation, buried alive in a purpose-built, concrete bunker. All day, tortured by heatstroke, hunger and fear, the men waited as the German commandant and his SS assistant walked between the ranks to select, quite arbitrarily, the chosen ten. As the commandant pointed to one man, Francis Gajowniczek, he cried out in despair, "My poor wife and children." At that moment the unimpressive figure of a man with sunken eyes and round glasses in wire frames stepped out of line and took off his cap. "What does this Polish pig want?" asked the commandant.

"I am a Catholic priest; I want to die for that man. I am old, he has a wife and children . . . I have no one," said Father Maximilian Kolbe.

"Accepted," retorted the commandant, before moving on.

That night, nine men and one priest went to the starvation bunker. Normally they would tear each other apart like cannibals.

Not so this time. While they had strength, lying naked on the floor, the men prayed and sang psalms. After two weeks, three of the men and Father Maximilian were still alive. The bunker was required for others, so on August 14, the remaining four were disposed of. At 12:50 P.M., after two weeks in the starvation bunker and still conscious, the Polish priest was finally given an injection of carbolic acid and died at the age of forty-seven.

On October 10, 1982 in St. Peter's Square, Rome, Father Maximilian's death was put in its proper perspective. Present in the crowd of 150,000, including twenty-six cardinals and three hundred bishops and archbishops, was Francis Gajowniczek and his family—for indeed, many had been saved by that one man. The Pope, describing Father Maximilian's death, said, "This was a victory won over all the systems of contempt and hate in man—a victory like that won by our Lord Jesus Christ."

When Francis Gajowniczek died, aged 94, I read his obituary in the Independent. He had spent the rest of his life going around telling people what Maximilian Kolbe had done for him, dying in his place. Jesus' death was even more amazing because it was not just for one man, but for every single person in the world.

Jesus came as our substitute. He endured crucifixion for us. Cicero described crucifixion as "the most cruel and hideous of tortures." Jesus was stripped and tied to a whipping post. He was flogged with four or five thongs of leather interwoven with sharp jagged bone and lead. Eusebius, the third-century church historian, described Roman flogging in these terms: the sufferer's "veins were laid bare, and . . . the very muscles, sinews and bowels of the victim were open to exposure." He was then taken to Pilate's headquarters where a crown of thorns was thrust onto His head. He was mocked by a battalion of about 600 men and hit about the face and head. He was then forced to carry a heavy cross bar on His bleeding shoulders until He collapsed, and Simon of Cyrene was forced into carrying it for Him.

When they reached the site of crucifixion, He was again stripped naked. He was laid on the cross, and six-inch nails were driven into His forearms, just above the wrist. His knees were twisted sideways so that the ankles could be nailed between the tibia and the Achilles' tendon. He was lifted up on the cross which was then dropped into a socket in the ground. There He was left to hang in intense heat and unbearable thirst, exposed to the ridicule of the crowd. He hung there in unthinkable pain for six hours while His life slowly drained away. It was the height of pain and the depth of shame.

Yet the worst part of His suffering was not the physical agony of torture and crucifixion, nor even the emotional pain of being rejected by the world and deserted by His friends, but the spiritual agony, cut off from His Father as He carried our sins.

Jesus' victory was total—He died not just for one person but for all of us—and it was also costly. In all four Gospels, we hear of Jesus' agony in the Garden of Gethsemane, alone, crying out to His Father, "Abba, Father . . . take this cup from me. Yet not what I will, but what you will" (Mark 14:36).

Raniero Cantalamessa writes:

> In the Bible the image of the cup almost always evokes the idea of God's wrath against sin . . . Wherever sin exists, God's judgment cannot but be focused on it, otherwise God would reach a compromise with sin and the very distinction itself between good and evil would no longer exist. Now, Jesus . . . is . . . man "made sin." Christ, it is written, died "for sinners;" he died in their place and not only in their favor . . . he is, therefore, "responsible" for all, the guilty one before God! It is against him that God's wrath is "revealed" and that is what "drinking the cup" means.[30]

The result

The cross is like a beautiful diamond, with many facets. From whichever angle you look at it you can see different colors and lights. The cross in a sense is a mystery; it is something too profound for understanding. However, from whichever angle you look at the cross you will never fathom its full depth and beauty. In the New Testament these angles are explored.

First, the cross shows just how much God loves us. If you are ever in any doubt that God loves us, look at the cross. Jesus said, "Greater love has no one than this, that he lay down his life for his friends" (John 15:13). The cross also tells us something about the nature of God. Probably the biggest question people ask about Christianity is: How can God allow so much suffering in the world? There are no simple answers to this difficult question but we do know this: God Himself is not aloof from suffering. He has come in the person of His Son, He suffered for us, and He now suffers alongside us. On the cross Jesus sets us an example of self-sacrificial love (1 Peter 2:21). The cross and the resurrection, which are in a sense one event, tell us that the powers of death and evil have been defeated (Colossians 2:15).

Each of these aspects deserves a chapter of its own, which space does not allow. However, I do want to concentrate here on four images that the New Testament uses to describe what Jesus did on the cross for us.[31] As John Stott, well-known author and Rector Emeritus of All Souls, Langham Place, points out, each of them is taken from a different area of day-to-day life.

The first image comes from the *temple*. In the Old Testament, very careful laws were laid down as to how sins should be dealt with. There was a whole system of sacrifices which demonstrated the seriousness of sin and the need for cleansing from it.

In a typical case the sinner would take an animal. The animal was to be as near perfection as possible. The sinner would lay his hands on the animal and confess his sins. Thus the sins were seen to pass from the sinner to the animal which was then killed.

The writer of Hebrews points out that it is "impossible for the blood of bulls and goats to take away sins" (Hebrews 10:4). It was only a picture or a "shadow" (Hebrews 10:1). The reality came with the sacrifice of Jesus. Only the blood of Christ, our substitute, can take away our sin. When John the Baptist saw Jesus he said "Look, the lamb of God, who takes away the sin of the world!" (John 1:29). He alone was the perfect sacrifice since He alone lived a perfect life. Jesus' blood purifies us from all sin (1 John 1:7). It washes away and removes *the pollution of sin.*

The second image comes from the *marketplace.* Debt is not a problem confined to the present day; it was a problem in the ancient world as well. If someone had serious debts, he might be forced to sell himself into slavery in order to pay them off. Suppose a man was standing in the marketplace, offering himself as a slave. Someone might have pity on him and ask, "How much do you owe?" The debtor might say, "$10,000." Suppose the customer offers to pay the $10,000 and then lets him go free. In doing so, he would be "redeeming him" by paying a "ransom price." In a similar way for us "redemption . . . came by Jesus Christ" (Romans 3:24). Jesus by His death on the cross paid the ransom price (Mark 10:45).

In this way, we are set free from the power of sin. This is true freedom. Jesus said, "If the Son sets you free, you will be free indeed" (John 8:36). When I became a Christian I was instantly set free from some things, but in other areas it has been a continual struggle. It is not that we never sin again, but that sin's hold over us is broken.

Billy Nolan ran away from the merchant navy and was an alcoholic for thirty-eight years. For twenty years he sat outside Holy Trinity Brompton, our church, drinking alcohol and begging for money. On May 13, 1990 he looked in the mirror and said to himself, "You're not the Billy Nolan I once knew." To use his own expression, he asked the Lord Jesus Christ into his life and made a covenant with Him that he would never drink alcohol again. He has not touched a drop since. His life is transformed. He radiates the love and joy of Christ. I once said to him, "Billy, you look happy." He replied, "I am happy because I am free. Life is like a maze and at last I have found a way out through Jesus Christ." Jesus' death on the cross made this freedom from *the power of sin* possible.

The third image comes from a *court of law.* Paul says that through Christ's death "we have been justified" (Romans 5:1). Justification is a legal term. If you went to court and were acquitted, you were justified. There is one illustration that particularly helped me to understand what this means.

Two people went through school and university together and developed a close friendship. Life went on and they went their different ways and lost contact. One went on to become a judge, while the other one went down and down and ended up a criminal. One day the criminal appeared before the judge. He had committed a crime to which he pleaded guilty. The judge recognized his old friend, and faced a dilemma. He was a judge so he had to be just; he couldn't let the man off. On the other hand, he didn't want to punish the man, because he loved him. So he told his friend that he would fine him the correct penalty for the offense. That is justice. Then he came down from his position as judge and he wrote a check for the amount of the fine. He gave it to his friend, saying that he would pay the penalty for him. That is love.

This is an illustration of what God has done for us. In His justice, He judges us because we are guilty, but then, in His love, He came down in the person of His Son Jesus Christ and paid the penalty for us. In this way He is both "just" (in that He does not allow the

guilty to go unpunished) and "the one who justifies"—Romans 3:26 (in that by taking the penalty Himself, in the person of His Son, He enables us to go free). He is both our Judge and our Savior. It is not an innocent third party but God Himself who saves us. In effect, He gives us a check and says we have a choice: do we want Him to pay it for us or are we going to face the judgment of God for our own wrong-doing?

The illustration I have used is not an exact one for three reasons. First, our plight is worse. The penalty we are facing is not just a fine, but death. Secondly, the relationship is closer. This is not just two friends: it is our Father in heaven who loves us more than any earthly parent loves their own child. Thirdly, the cost was greater: it cost God not money, but His one and only Son—who paid the *penalty of sin.*

The fourth image comes from the *home.* We saw that both the root and the result of sin were a broken relationship with God. The result of the cross is the possibility of a restored relationship with God. Paul says that "God *was* reconciling the world to himself in Christ" (2 Corinthians 5:19, italics mine). Some people caricature the New Testament teaching and suggest that God is barbaric and unjust because He punished Jesus, an innocent party, instead of us. This is not what the New Testament says. Rather, Paul says, "God was . . . in Christ." He was Himself the substitute in the person of His Son. He made it possible for us to be restored to a relationship with Him. The *partition of sin* has been destroyed; "the temple curtain was torn in two from top to bottom" (Matthew 27:51).

What happened to the Prodigal Son can happen to us. We can come back to the Father and experience His love and blessing. The relationship is not only for this life: it is eternal. One day we will be with the Father in a heaven and earth made new—there we will be free, not only from the penalty of sin, the power of sin, the pollution of sin, and the partition of sin, but also from the presence of sin. That is what God has made possible through His self-substitution on the cross.

God loves each one of us so much and longs to be in a relationship with us as a human parent longs to be in a relationship with each of their children. It is not just that Jesus died for everyone. He died for you and for me; it is intensely personal. Paul writes of "the Son of God, who loved me and gave himself for me" (Galatians 2:20). If you had been the only person in the world, Jesus would have died for you. As St. Augustine put it, "he died for every one of us as if there were only one of us." Once we see the cross in these personal terms, our lives will be transformed.

John Wimber, an American pastor and church leader, described how the cross became a personal reality to him:

> After I had studied the Bible for about three months I could have passed an elementary exam on the cross. I understood there is one God who could be known in three Persons. I understood Jesus is fully God and fully man and he died on the cross for the sins of the world. But I didn't understand that I was a sinner. I thought I was a good guy. I knew I messed up here and there but I didn't realize how serious my condition was.
>
> But one evening around this time Carol [his wife] said, "I think it's time to do something about all that we've been learning." Then, as I looked on in utter amazement, she knelt down on the floor and started praying to what seemed to me to be the ceiling plaster. "Oh God," she said, "I am sorry for my sin."
>
> I couldn't believe it. Carol was a better person than I, yet she thought she was a sinner. I could feel her pain and the depth of her prayers. Soon she was weeping and repeating, "I am sorry for my sin." There were six or seven people in the room, all with their eyes closed.

I looked at them and then it hit me: They've all prayed this prayer too! I started sweating bullets. I thought I was going to die. The perspiration ran down my face and I thought, "I'm not going to do this. This is dumb. I'm a good guy." Then it struck me. Carol wasn't praying to the plaster; she was praying to a person, to a God who could hear her. In comparison to Him she knew she was a sinner in need of forgiveness.

In a flash the cross made personal sense to me. Suddenly I knew something that I had never known before; I had hurt God's feelings. He loved me and in His love for me He sent Jesus. But I had turned away from that love; I had shunned it all of my life. I was a sinner, desperately in need of the cross.

Then I too was kneeling on the floor, sobbing, nose running, eyes watering, every square inch of my flesh perspiring profusely. I had this overwhelming sense that I was talking with someone who had been with me all of my life, but whom I failed to recognize. Like Carol, I began talking to the living God, telling Him that I was a sinner but the only words I could say aloud were, "Oh God, Oh God."

I knew something revolutionary was going on inside of me. I thought, "I hope this works, because I'm making a complete fool of myself." Then the Lord brought to mind a man I had seen in Pershing Square in Los Angeles a number of years before. He was wearing a sign that said, "I'm a fool for Christ. Whose fool are you?" I thought at the time, "That's the most stupid thing I've ever seen." But as I kneeled on the floor I realized the truth of the odd sign: the cross is foolishness "to those who are perishing" (1 Corinthians 1:18). That night I knelt at the cross and believed in Jesus. I've been a fool for Christ ever since.[32]

CHAPTER 4

HOW CAN WE HAVE FAITH?

Some people are at their best in the morning, others come to life at night. My best time of day is first thing. I wake up full of energy but as the day goes on I begin to fade. By nine o'clock at night I am ready to go to bed. By ten o'clock I am falling asleep. By eleven o'clock I am asleep, wherever I happen to be!

"Midnight feasts aren't his thing."

I have always been like that, even when I was at university. At the end of my last term there I attended our college ball. That evening I met a girl whom I had talked to a couple of times before. She was about the same age as me. We started chatting and then we danced. Eleven o'clock came and went. Three o'clock came and went. Five o'clock came and went. At seven o'clock in the morning we started playing tennis. Then we went boating on the river and afterwards had lunch. I hadn't had a moment's sleep, but I didn't feel remotely tired. Word quickly spread among my friends that I was definitely going to marry this girl because I had been up after eleven o'clock at night. And they were right—Pippa and I were married two years later!

That night a new life had begun—I was never the same again. Similarly, becoming a Christian is the start of a new life. Relationships are exciting but the most exciting relationship of all is our relationship with God. As Paul wrote, "those who become Christians become new persons. They are not the same any more for the old is gone. A new life has begun!" (2 Corinthians 5:17, New Living Translation). I sometimes keep a note of what people say or write after they have begun the new life that Paul is speaking about. For example:

> I now have hope where previously there was only despair. I can forgive now, where before there was only coldness ... God is so alive for me. I can feel Him guiding me and the complete and utter loneliness which I have been feeling is gone. God is filling a deep, deep void.
>
> I had met other Christians (through a friend) who just seemed very at peace with the world and fulfilled and I thought I fancy a bit of that ... I found God and became a Christian during the Alpha course ... I feel at peace and happier with life and am searching for ways to strengthen my relationship with God.

When St. Paul refers to people becoming Christians, what does he mean? What is a Christian? The word Christian, of course, can be used in many different ways in our society. However, originally a Christian was a *Christ*ian, a follower of Jesus; someone who has a relationship with God through His son.

Experiences of how that relationship begins vary greatly. Some people know the exact date on which they became a Christian, as I do. Some would say, "I can never remember a time when I wasn't a Christian." Others might say, "I think there was a time when I wasn't a Christian. I am a Christian now, but it was a process and I couldn't tell you exactly when it happened." What matters is not so much the experience as the fact that when we receive Christ, we become a child of God. As the apostle John writes, "Yet to all who received him, to those who believed in his name, he gave the right to become children of God" (John 1:12). C. S. Lewis used this analogy: on a train from Paris to Berlin, some people will be awake at the moment the train crosses the border. These passengers will know the exact moment that it happened. Others will be asleep. What matters is that they know they've arrived in Berlin.

Many people are uncertain about whether they are Christians or not. I ask people at the end of Alpha courses to fill in questionnaires. One of the questions I ask is, "Would you have described yourself as a Christian at the beginning of the course?" Here is a list of some of the answers:

"Yes, but without any real experience of a relationship with God."
"Sort of."
"Possibly yes/think so."
"Not sure."
"Probably."
"Ish."
"Yes—though looking back possibly no."
"No, a semi-Christian."

The New Testament makes it clear that it is possible for us to be sure that we are Christians and that we have eternal life. The apostle John writes, "I write these things to you who believe in the name of the Son of God so that you may *know* that you have eternal life" (1 John 5:13, italics mine).

How can we know that we have been given eternal life? Just as three legs support a camera tripod, the assurance of our relationship with God stands firmly based on the activity of all three members of the Trinity: the promises which the Father gives us in His word, the sacrifice of the Son for us on the cross, and the assurance of the Spirit in our hearts. These can be summarized under three headings: the Word of God, the work of Jesus, and the witness of the Holy Spirit.

The Word of God

If you asked me how I know I'm married, one answer I could give would be to show you a particular document, our marriage certificate.

This is a piece of evidence that proves the fact that Pippa and I are married. If you asked me how I know I am a Christian, one answer I could give would be to show you a document, the Bible.

The first leg of the tripod is the Word of God. Our knowledge of God is based on the promises in the Bible. It is based on facts, not feelings. If we were to rely only on our feelings we could never be sure about anything. Our feelings go up and down depending on all sorts of factors, such as the weather or what we've had for breakfast. They can be changeable and even deceptive. The promises in the Bible, which is the Word of God, do not change and are totally reliable.

There are many great promises in the Bible. A verse that I found helpful, especially at the beginning of my Christian life, is one that comes in the last book of the Bible. In a vision St. John sees Jesus speaking to seven different churches. To the church in Laodicea Jesus says, "Here I am! I stand at the door and knock. If anyone hears my voice and opens the door, I will come in and eat with him, and he with me" (Revelation 3:20).

There are many ways of speaking about starting the new life of the Christian faith—"becoming a Christian," "giving our lives to Christ," "receiving Christ," "inviting Jesus into our lives," "believing in Him," and "opening the door to Jesus" are some of the variations. All of them describe the same reality; that Jesus enters our lives by the Holy Spirit, as is pictured in this verse.

The Pre-Raphaelite artist, Holman Hunt (1827–1910), inspired by this verse painted *The Light of the World*. He painted three versions in all. One hangs in Keble College, Oxford; another version is in the Manchester City Art Gallery; the most famous toured the world in 1905–7 and was presented to St. Paul's Cathedral in June 1908, where it still hangs. When the first version was shown it received generally poor reviews. Then, on May 5, 1854, John Ruskin, the artist and critic, wrote to *The Times* and explained the symbolism at length and brilliantly defended it as "one of the very noblest works of sacred art ever produced in this or any other age."

Jesus, the Light of the World, stands at a door, which is overgrown with ivy and weeds. The door represents the door of someone's life. This person has never invited Jesus to come into his or her life. Jesus is standing at the door and knocking. He is awaiting a response. He

wants to come in and be part of that person's life. Apparently, someone said to Holman Hunt that he had made a mistake. They told him, "You have forgotten to paint a handle on the door."

"Oh no," replied Hunt, "that is deliberate. There is only one handle and that is on the inside."

In other words, we have to open the door to let Jesus into our lives. Jesus will never force His way in. He gives us the freedom to choose. It is up to us whether or not we open the door to Him. If we do, He promises, "I will come in and eat with them and they with me." Eating together is a sign of the friendship which Jesus offers to all those who open the door of their lives to Him.

Once we have invited Jesus to come in, He promises that He will never leave us. He says to His disciples, "I am with you always" (Matthew 28:20). We may not always be in direct conversation with Him, but He will always be there. If you are working in a room with a friend, you may not be talking to each other all the time, but you are nevertheless aware of each other's presence. This is how it is with the presence of Jesus. He is with us always.

This promise of the presence of Jesus with us is closely related to another extraordinary promise, which comes in the New Testament. Jesus promises to give His followers eternal life (John 10:28). As we have seen, "eternal life" in the New Testament is a quality of life that comes from being in a relationship with God through Jesus Christ (John 17:3). It starts now, when we experience the fullness of life which Jesus came to bring (John 10:10). Yet it is not just for this life; it goes on into eternity.

The resurrection of Jesus from the dead has many implications. First, it assures us about the *past*, that what Jesus achieved on the cross was effective. "The resurrection is not the reversal of a defeat, but the proclamation of a victory."[33] Second, it assures us about the *present*; Jesus is alive. His power is with us, bringing us life in all its fullness. Third, it assures us about the *future*. This life is not the end; there is life beyond the grave. History is not meaningless or cyclical; it is moving towards a glorious climax.

One day Jesus will return to earth to establish a new heaven and a new earth (Revelation 21:1). Then those who are in Christ will go to "be with the Lord for ever" (1 Thessalonians 4:17). There will be no more crying, for there will be no more pain. There will be no more temptation, for there will be no more sin. There will be no more suffering and no more separation from loved ones. Then we will see Jesus face to face (1 Corinthians 13:12). We will be given glorious and painless resurrection bodies (1 Corinthians 15). We will be transformed into the moral likeness of Jesus Christ (1 John 3:2). Heaven will be a place of intense joy and delight which goes on forever. Some have ridiculed this by suggesting it would be monotonous or boring. But: "No eye has seen, no ear has heard, no mind has conceived what God has prepared for those who love him" (1 Corinthians 2:9 quoting Isaiah 64:4).

As C. S. Lewis put it in one of his Narnia books:

> The term is over: the holidays have begun. The dream is ended: this is the morning . . . all their life in this world . . . had only been the cover and the title page: now at last they were beginning Chapter One of the Great Story which no one on earth has read: which goes on forever: in which every chapter is better than the one before.[34]

The work of Jesus

To the question how do I know I'm married, I could show you the marriage certificate. I could also point you to an event that took place on January 7, 1978, our wedding. Similarly, if you asked me how I know I'm a Christian, I could also point to an event in history; the death and resurrection of Jesus Christ.

Therefore, the second leg of the tripod is the work of Jesus. The wonderful news is that our confidence in eternal life is based not on what we do or achieve, but on what Jesus has done for us. What He did on the cross enables us to receive eternal life as a gift (John 10:28). We do not earn a gift. We accept it with gratitude.

It all starts with God's love for us: "For God so loved the world that he gave his one and only Son, that whoever believes in him shall not perish but have eternal life' (John 3:16). We all deserve to "perish." God, in His love for us, saw the mess we were in and gave His only Son, Jesus, to die for us. As a result of His death, everlasting life is offered to all who believe.

On the cross, Jesus took all our wrong-doing upon Himself. This had been clearly prophesied in the Old Testament. In the Book of Isaiah, written hundreds of years beforehand, the prophet foresaw what "the suffering servant" would do for us and said: "We all, like sheep, have gone astray, each of us has turned to his own way; and the Lord has laid on him [i.e., Jesus] the iniquity of us all" (Isaiah 53:6).

What the prophet is saying is that we have all done wrong—we have all gone astray. He says elsewhere that the things that we do wrong cause a separation between us and God (Isaiah 59:1-2). This is one of the reasons why God can seem remote. There is a barrier between us and Him which prevents us from experiencing His love.

On the other hand, Jesus never did anything wrong. He lived a perfect life. There was no barrier between Him and His Father. On the cross, God transferred our wrong-doings ("our iniquity") onto Jesus ("the Lord has laid on him the iniquity of us all"). That is why Jesus cried out on the cross, "My God, my God, why have you forsaken me?" (Mark 15:34). At that moment He was cut off from God—not because of His own wrong-doing, but because of ours.

I am slightly cynical when I hear of a "free gift." Eternal life is a free gift unlike any other and although free for us, it cost Jesus His life. We receive this gift through repentance and faith.

What is repentance? The Greek word for "repentance" means changing our minds. If we want to receive this gift, we have to be willing to turn from everything we know to be wrong. These are the things which do us harm and lead to "death" (Romans 6:23a). C. S. Lewis said repentance was like "laying down your arms, surrendering, saying you are sorry, realizing that you have been on the wrong track and being ready to start life over again from the ground floor."

What is faith? Blondin was a famous tightrope walker and acrobat in the nineteenth century. Large crowds used to watch him, particularly when he was crossing the Niagara Falls. His act began with a relatively simple crossing using a balancing pole. Then he would throw the pole away and begin to amaze the onlookers. On one occasion in 1860, a Royal party from Britain went to watch him perform. He crossed the tightrope on stilts, then blindfolded; next he stopped halfway to cook and eat an omelet. He then wheeled a wheelbarrow from one side to the other as the crowd cheered. He put a sack of potatoes into the wheelbarrow and wheeled that across. The crowd cheered louder. Then he approached the Royal party and asked the Duke of Newcastle, "Do you believe that I could take a man across the tightrope in this wheelbarrow?"

"Yes, I do," said the Duke.

"Hop in!" replied Blondin. The crowd fell silent, but the Duke of Newcastle would not accept his challenge. No one was willing to volunteer. Eventually, an old woman stepped out of the crowd and climbed into the wheelbarrow. Blondin wheeled her all the way across and all the way back. The old woman was Blondin's mother, the only person willing to put her life in his hands. Faith in this sense is "hopping in." It isn't merely an intellectual exercise; it involves an active step of putting our trust in Jesus.

When we repent and believe, we can be sure of God's forgiveness and know our guilt has been taken away. We can also be sure that we will never be condemned. As Paul puts it, "Therefore, there is now no condemnation for those who are in Christ Jesus" (Romans 8:1). This, then, is the second reason we can be sure that we have eternal life—because of what Jesus achieved for us on the cross by dying for us.

The witness of the Spirit

To prove that I am married, as well as a document and an event, I could also point you to the experience of many years of marriage. To show how I know I am a Christian I can point to a document, to an event that took place in history, and third to the experience of the Holy Spirit. When someone becomes a Christian, God's Holy Spirit comes to live within them. There are two aspects of this experience that help us to be sure of our faith in Christ.

First, He transforms us from within. He produces the character of Jesus in our lives. This is called "the fruit of the Spirit"—"love, joy, peace, patience, kindness, goodness, faithfulness, gentleness and self-control" (Galatians 5:22-23). When the Holy Spirit comes to live within us this "fruit" begins to grow.

There will be changes in our character that should be observable by other people, but obviously these changes do not occur overnight. We once planted a pear tree in our garden and almost every day I used to look excitedly to see if any fruit had appeared. One day a friend of mine (the illustrator of this book) hung a large Granny Smith apple on the tree with a piece of string. Upon closer examination, even I was not fooled by this! From my limited knowledge of gardening I know that fruit takes time to grow and pear trees do not produce apples. It's over a period of time that the Holy Spirit transforms us to be more loving, more joyful, more peaceful, more patient, more kind, more self-controlled.

As well as changes in our character there should be changes in our relationships, both with God and with other people. We develop a new love for God—Father, Son, and Holy Spirit. For example, hearing the word "Jesus" has a different emotional impact. Before I was a Christian, to me, the word "Jesus" was just a swear word. If I heard His name on the radio or on the television I would usually switch channels, as I was not very interested in religion. After I became a Christian, however, I would turn it up because my attitude to Jesus had completely changed. This was a little sign of my new love for Him.

Our attitude to others also changes. Often, new Christians say that they begin to notice the faces of people in the street and on the bus. Before, they had little interest; now they feel sympathy for people who look sad or lonely. I found that one of the biggest differences was in my attitude to other Christians. Before, I tended to avoid anyone who had a Christian faith. Afterwards, I found they weren't as bad as I had expected! Indeed, I started to experience a depth of friendship with other Christians that I had never known in my life before.

Secondly, the Holy Spirit also brings an inner experience of God. He creates a deep, personal conviction that we are children of God (Romans 8:15-16).

I have three children, who are now grown up. In my opinion many children are overworked during their time at school. The main advice I used to give my children was, "Don't work so hard!" Whatever was said in my children's school reports, I thought they were fantastic. I remember looking at my thirteen-year-old daughter's report card, which I (of course) thought was wonderful. She, however, pointed out areas in which she was disappointed, and said that she should have done better in French, and so on. My response was, "I don't really care how you did in French. I think you're fantastic. In fact, I wouldn't really care if your whole report card was bad; I love you because I love you." Later that evening, as I thought about our conversation, I sensed God saying to me, "This is how I feel about you."

The love of God for each one of us is far greater than the love of human parents for their children. I often feel that I could do better, that I am not good at one thing or another, and that I fail again and again. Yet God accepts us and loves us simply because He loves us. We know this because the Spirit of God witnesses to us—both objectively through an ongoing change in our character and in our relationships, and subjectively through a deep inner conviction that we are children of God.

In these ways (the Word of God, the work of Jesus and the witness of the Spirit), those who believe in Jesus can be sure that they are children of God and that they have eternal life.

It is not arrogant to be sure that we have eternal life. It is based on what God has promised, on what Jesus died to achieve, and on the work of the Holy Spirit in our lives. It is one of the privileges of being a child of God that we can be absolutely confident about our relationship with our Father, that we can know His forgiveness and be sure that we are Christians and that we have eternal life.

If you are unsure about whether you have ever really believed in Jesus, here is a prayer that you can pray as a way of starting the Christian life and receiving all the benefits which Christ died to make possible.

> Heavenly Father, I am sorry for the things I have done wrong in my life. [Take a few moments to ask His forgiveness for anything particular that is on your conscience.] Please forgive me. I now turn from everything that I know is wrong.
>
> Thank You that you sent Your Son, Jesus, to die on the cross for me so that I could be forgiven and set free. From now on I will follow and obey Him as my Lord.
>
> Thank You that You now offer me this gift of forgiveness and Your Spirit. I now receive that gift.
>
> Please come into my life by Your Holy Spirit to be with me for ever. Through Jesus Christ, our Lord. Amen.

CHAPTER 5

WHY AND HOW DO I PRAY?

Surveys have shown that three-quarters of the population of skeptical, secular Britain admit to praying at least once a week. Before I became a Christian I prayed two different types of prayers. First, I prayed a prayer I was taught as a child by my grandmother (who was not herself a churchgoer), "God bless Mummy and Daddy . . . and everybody and make me a good boy. Amen." There was nothing wrong with the prayer, but for me it was only a formula, which I prayed every night before I went to sleep, with superstitious fears about what might go wrong if I didn't.

Secondly, I prayed in times of crisis. For example, at the age of seventeen I was traveling by myself in the United States. The bus company managed to lose my backpack, which contained my clothes, money, and address book. I was left with virtually nothing. I spent ten days living on a hippie colony in Key West, sharing a tent with an alcoholic. After that, with a feeling of mounting loneliness and desperation, I spent the days wandering around various American cities and the nights on the bus. One day as I walked along the street, I cried out to God (in whom I did not believe) and prayed that I would meet someone I knew. Not long afterwards, I got on the bus at 6 A.M. in Phoenix, Arizona, and there I saw an old school friend. He lent me some money and we traveled together for a few days. It made all the difference. I did not see it as an answer to prayer, only as a coincidence. Since becoming a Christian I have found that it is remarkable how many "coincidences" happen when we pray.

What is prayer?

Prayer is the most important activity of our lives because it is the main way in which we develop a relationship with our Father in heaven. Jesus said, "When you pray, go into your room, close the door and pray to your Father, who is unseen" (Matthew 6:6). It is natural for human beings to want to communicate with God, and Jesus shows us how. He sees prayer as a relationship rather than a ritual. It is not a torrent of mechanical and mindless words. Indeed, Jesus said, "Do not keep on babbling like pagans" (Matthew 6:7). Prayer is a conversation with our Father in heaven. So it is a matter of relationship, and when we pray the whole Trinity is involved—Father, Son, and Holy Spirit.

Christian prayer is prayer "to your Father"

Jesus taught us to pray, "Our Father in heaven" (Matthew 6:9). God is personal. Of course He is "beyond personality" as C. S. Lewis put it, but He is nevertheless personal. We are made in the image of God. He is our loving Father and we have the extraordinary privilege of being able to come into His presence and call Him "Abba"—the Aramaic word for which the nearest translation is "Daddy" or "Dear Father." There is a remarkable intimacy about our relationship with God and about praying to our Father in heaven.

He is not only "our Father," He is "our Father in heaven." He has heavenly power. When we pray we are speaking to the Creator of the universe. On August 20, 1977, Voyager II, the inter-planetary probe launched to observe and transmit to earth data about the outer planetary system, set off from earth traveling faster than the speed of a bullet at 90,000 miles per hour. On August 28, 1989 it reached planet Neptune, 2,700 million miles from the earth. Voyager II then left the solar system. It will not come within one light year of any star for 958,000 years. In our galaxy there are 100,000 million stars, like our sun. Our galaxy is one of 100,000 million galaxies. In a throwaway line in Genesis, the writer tells us, "He also made the stars" (Genesis 1:16). Such is His power. Andrew Murray, the Christian writer, once said, "The power of prayer depends almost entirely upon our apprehension of who it is with whom we speak."[35]

When we pray, we are speaking to a God who is both transcendent and immanent. He is far greater and more powerful than the universe that He created and yet He is there with us when we pray.

Christian prayer is "through the Son"

Paul says that "through him [Jesus] we . . . have access to the Father by one Spirit" (Ephesians 2:18). Jesus said that His Father would give "whatever you ask in my name" (John 15:16). We have no right in ourselves to come to God but we are able to do so "through Jesus" and "in his name." That is why it is customary to end prayers with "through Jesus Christ our Lord" or "in the name of Jesus." This is not just a formula, it is our acknowledgement of the fact that we can only come to God through Jesus. It is Jesus, through His death on the cross, who removed the barrier between us and God. He is our great High Priest. That is why there is such power in the name of Jesus.

The value of a check depends not only on the amount, but also on the name that appears at the bottom. If I wrote out a check for ten million dollars it would be worthless; but if Bill Gates, one of the richest men in the world, were to write a check for ten million dollars it would be worth exactly that. When we go to the bank of heaven, we have nothing deposited there. If I go in my own name I can achieve nothing; but Jesus Christ has unlimited credit in heaven and He has given us the privilege of using His name.

Christian prayer is prayer "by one Spirit" (Ephesians 2:18)

We can find it hard to pray, but God has not left us without help. He has given us His Spirit to live within us and help us to pray. Paul writes, "In the same way, the Spirit helps us in our weakness. We do not know what we ought to pray for, but the Spirit himself intercedes for us with groans that words cannot express. And he who searches our hearts knows the mind of the Spirit, because the Spirit intercedes for the saints in accordance with God's will" (Romans 8:26-27). In a later chapter we shall look in more detail at the work of the Spirit. Here, it is sufficient to note that when we pray, God helps us to pray by His Spirit who lives in us as Christians.

Why pray?

Prayer is a vital activity. There are many reasons for praying. In the first place it is the way in which we develop a relationship with our Father in heaven. Sometimes people say, "God knows our needs, so why do we have to ask?" Well, it would not be much of a relationship if there was no communication. Of course, asking is not the only way in which we communicate with God. There are other forms of prayer: thanksgiving, praise, adoration, confession, listening, and so on. But asking is an important part. As we ask God for things and see our prayers answered, our trust in Him deepens.

Jesus prayed, and taught us to do the same. He had an uninterrupted relationship with His Father. His life was one of constant prayer. There are numerous references to His praying, and in the Bible we read that Jesus often withdrew to pray (e.g., Mark 1:35; Luke 6:12).

Jesus also says that when we pray God will reward us. We might ask whether it is appropriate to be looking for a reward. Of course there are inappropriate rewards: money for sex is an inappropriate reward. But there are also appropriate rewards. If someone is working hard for their exams, then passing them, receiving a good grade is an appropriate reward. C. S. Lewis put it like this, "The proper rewards are not simply tacked onto the activity for which they are given, but are the activity itself in consummation."[36]

Many of us feel an underlying restlessness or a sense of sadness or yearning, and in my experience, prayer satisfies this spiritual hunger. The reward is that when we pray, we begin to experience God's love for us and His presence with us. The psalmist says, "In your presence is fullness of joy" (Psalm 16:11, NKJV).

Finally, prayer not only changes us but it also changes situations. Many people can accept that the act of praying in itself will have a beneficial effect on themselves, but some have philosophical objections to the concept that prayer can make things happen, changing events and even third parties. Rabbi Daniel Cohn-Scherbok, formerly of the University of Kent, once wrote an article arguing that as God already knows the future it therefore must be fixed. To this Clifford Longley, the former Religious Affairs correspondent of *The Times*, correctly replied, "If God lives in the eternal present, he hears all prayers simultaneously. Therefore he can appropriate a prayer from next week, and attach it to an event a month ago."

Jesus often encouraged us to ask. He said, "Ask and it will be given to you; seek and you will find; knock and the door will be opened to you. For everyone who asks receives; he who seeks finds; and to him who knocks, the door will be opened" (Matthew 7:7-8).

Every Christian knows, through experience, that God answers prayer. When I started out, I began to pray for little things in my own life. Coincidences started to happen. Then, the more I prayed, the more coincidences I saw. I made a connection and I risked praying for bigger things. Of course, it is not possible to prove Christianity on the basis of answers to our own prayers because they can always be explained away by cynics. But the cumulative effective of answered prayer reinforces our faith in God. I have kept a prayer diary for years now and it is fascinating to me to see how day after day, week after week, year after year, God has answered my prayers.

Does God always answer prayer?

In the passage I have quoted from Matthew 7:7-8 and in many other New Testament passages the promises appear to be absolute. However, when we look at the whole of Scripture, we see there are good reasons why we may not always get what we ask for.

When we do not confess to God the things we have done wrong, it can cause a barrier between us and God: "Surely the arm of the Lord is not too short to save, nor his ear too dull to hear. But your iniquities have separated you from your God; your sins have hidden his face from you, so that he will not hear" (Isaiah 59:1-2). Of course, all of us get things wrong, and if this disqualified us from praying, no one would ever pray. But Jesus died on the cross so that we could be forgiven. This in turn enables us to pray. When people say, "I don't feel I am getting through to God. I don't feel there is anyone there," the first question to ask them is whether they have ever received God's forgiveness through Christ on the cross. The barrier must be removed before we can expect God to hear and answer our prayers.

Even as Christians our friendship with God can be marred by sin or disobedience. John writes, "Dear friends, if our hearts do not condemn us, we have confidence before God and receive from him anything we ask, because we obey his commands and do what pleases him" (1 John 3:21-22). If we are conscious of any sin or disobedience towards God, we need to confess it and turn from it so that our friendship with God can be restored and we can approach Him again with confidence. God sees everything—it is not possible to trick Him by planning simultaneously both the sin and the repentance.

Our motivation can also be a hindrance to getting what we ask for. Not every request to win the lottery, marry a Hollywood star, or own an Aston Martin will get answered! James, the brother of Jesus, writes:

> You want something but don't get it. You kill and covet, but you cannot have what you want. You quarrel and fight. You do not have, because you do not ask God. When you ask, you do not receive, because you ask with wrong motives, that you may spend what you get on your pleasures. (James 4:2-3)

A famous example of a prayer riddled with wrong motives is that of John Ward of Hackney, written in the eighteenth century:

> O Lord, thou knowest that I have nine estates in the City of London, and likewise that I have lately purchased one estate in fee simple in the county of Essex; I beseech thee to preserve the two counties of Essex and Middlesex from fire and earthquake; and as I have a mortgage in Hertfordshire, I beg of thee likewise to have an eye of compassion on that county; and for the rest of the counties thou mayest deal with them as thou art pleased.
>
> O Lord, enable the bank to answer their bills, and make all my debtors good men. Give a prosperous voyage and return to the Mermaid ship, because I have insured it; and as thou hast said that the days of the wicked are but short, I trust in thee, that thou wilt not forget thy promise, as I have purchased an estate in reversion which will be mine on the death of that profligate young man, Sir J. L.
>
> Keep my friends from sinking, and preserve me from thieves and house breakers, and make all my servants so honest and faithful that they may attend to my interests, and never cheat me out of my property, night or day.

John writes, "If we ask anything *according to his will*, he hears us" (1 John 5:14, italics mine). The more we get to know God, the better we will know His will and the more our prayers will be answered.

Sometimes prayers are not answered because what we are requesting is not good for us. God only promises to give us "good gifts" (Matthew 7:11). He loves us and knows what is best for us. Good parents do not always give their children what they ask for. If a two-year-old wants to play with a carving knife, a good parent will say "no." As John Stott has written, God will answer "no" if the things we ask for are "either not good in themselves, or not good for us or for others, directly or indirectly, immediately or ultimately."

The answer to our prayer will either be "yes," "no" or sometimes "wait," and for this we should be extremely grateful. If we were given carte blanche we would never dare pray again. Ruth Graham (married to Billy Graham, author and evangelist) told an audience in Minneapolis, "God has not always answered my prayers. If he had, I would have married the wrong man—several times!"

In my experience, it sometimes seems almost as if God has hidden His face from us. The psalmist, "How long, O Lord? Will you forget me forever? How long will you hide your face from me?" (Psalm 13:1). At times like this we need to trust God despite the silence. As the psalmist puts it, "But I trust in your unfailing love; my heart rejoices in your salvation" (Psalm 13:5).

Sometimes we will not know during this life why the answer is "no." I can think of an occasion in 1996 when I was playing squash with one of my closest friends, Mick Hawkins, a man of forty-two with six children. In the middle of the game he dropped dead from a heart attack. I have never cried out to God more than I did on that occasion; asking Him to heal him, restore him, and praying that the heart attack would not be fatal. I do not know why he died.

That night I couldn't sleep, so I got up at about 5 o'clock in the morning. I went out for a walk and said to the Lord, "I don't understand why Mick died. He was such an amazing person, such a wonderful husband and father. I don't understand . . ." Then I realized I had a choice. I could say, "I am going to stop believing." However, the alternative was to say, "I am going to go on believing in spite of the fact that I don't understand and I am going to trust you, Lord, even though I don't think I will ever understand—in this life—why this happened."

There may be times when we will have to wait until we meet God face to face to understand what His will was and why our prayer did not get the answer we hoped for.[37]

How should we pray?

There is no set way to pray. Prayer is an integral part of our relationship with God and therefore we are free to talk to Him as we wish. God does not want us to repeat meaningless words or religious jargon; He wants us to be honest with Him and to say what is on our hearts. Many people find it helpful to have a pattern for prayer. For some years I used the acronym ACTS.

A – Adoration—praising God for who He is and what He has done.
C – Confession—asking God's forgiveness for anything that we have done wrong.
T – Thanksgiving—for health, family, friends, and so on.
S – Supplication—asking for certain things or outcomes for ourselves, for our friends, and for others.

More recently I have tended to follow the pattern of the Lord's Prayer (Matthew 6:9-13):

"Our Father in heaven" (v. 9)

We have already looked earlier in this chapter at what this phrase means. Under this heading, I spend time thanking God for who He is and for my relationship with Him and for the ways in which He has answered prayers.

"Hallowed be your name" (v. 9)

In Hebrew someone's name signified a revelation of that person's character. To pray that God's name be hallowed is to pray that He will be honored. So often we look around our society and see that God's name is dishonored—many people pay no attention to Him or only use His name as a swear word. We should start by praying that God's name is honored in our own lives, in our families, in our workplaces, and in the society around us.

"Your kingdom come" (v. 10)

God's kingdom is His rule and reign. This will be complete when Jesus comes again. But this kingdom broke into history when Jesus came for the first time. Jesus demonstrated the presence of God's kingdom in His own ministry. When we pray, "Your kingdom come," we are praying for God's rule and reign to come both in the future and in the present. It includes praying for people to be converted, healed, set free from evil, filled with the Spirit and given the gifts of the Spirit, in order that we may together serve and obey the King.

I am told that the nineteenth-century preacher D. L. Moody wrote down a list of 100 people and prayed for them to be converted in his lifetime. Ninety-six of them had become Christians by the time he died and the other four came to faith at his funeral.

A young mother named Monica, who was a Christian, was having problems with her rebellious teenage son. He was lazy, bad-tempered, and dishonest. Later on, though outwardly respected as a lawyer, his life was dominated by ambition and a desire to make money. He lived with several different women and had a son by one of them. At one stage he even joined a weird religious sect. Throughout this time his mother continued to pray for him. One day, the Lord gave her a vision and she wept as she prayed, because she saw the light of Jesus Christ in him, and his face transformed. She had to wait another nine years before her son gave his life to Jesus Christ at the age of thirty-two. That man's name was Augustine. He came to faith in A.D. 386, was ordained in 391, made bishop in 396 and became one of the greatest theologians in the history of the church. He always attributed his conversion to the prayers of his mother.

We are praying not simply for God's rule and reign in individuals' lives but ultimately for the transformation of society. We are praying for God's peace, justice, and compassion. We are praying for those often marginalized by society but for whom God cares especially, such as widows, orphans, prisoners, and those who are lost and lonely (Psalm 68:4-6a).

"Your will be done on earth as it is in heaven" (v. 10)

This is not resignation, but a releasing of the burdens that we so often carry. Many people are worried about decisions they are facing. The decisions may be about major or minor issues but if we want to be sure that we don't make a mistake we need to pray, "Your will be done." The psalmist says, "Commit your way to the Lord; trust in him and he will act" (Psalm 37:5, RSV). For example, if you are praying about whether a relationship is right, you might pray, "If this relationship is wrong, I pray that you stop it. If it is right I pray that nothing will stop it." Then, having committed it to the Lord, you can trust Him and wait for Him to act.

"Give us today our daily bread" (v. 11)

Some have suggested that Jesus meant the spiritual bread of Holy Communion or the Bible. This is possible, but I believe the reformers were right to say that Jesus is referring here to our basic needs. Luther said it indicated "everything necessary for the preservation of this life, like food, a healthy body, good weather, house, home, wife, children, good government and peace." God is concerned about everything that you and I are concerned about. Just as I want my children to talk to me about anything they are worried about, so God wants to hear about the things we are concerned about.

A friend of mine asked a new Christian how her small business was going. She replied that it was not going very well. So my friend offered to pray for it. The new Christian replied, "I didn't know that was allowed." My friend explained that it was. They prayed and the following week the business improved considerably. The Lord's Prayer teaches us that it is not wrong to pray about our own concerns, provided that God's name, God's kingdom, and God's will are our first priority.

"Forgive us our debts, as we also have forgiven our debtors" (v. 12)

Jesus taught us to pray that God would forgive us our debts (the things we do wrong). Some say, "Why do we need to pray for forgiveness? Surely when we come to the cross we are forgiven for everything, past, present and future?" It is true, as we saw in chapter 3, that we are totally forgiven for everything, past, present, and future because Jesus took all our sins on Himself on the cross. Yet Jesus still tells us to pray, "Forgive us our debts." Why is this?

I find the most helpful analogy is the one given by Jesus in John 13 when Jesus moves to wash Peter's feet. Peter says, "No, you shall never wash my feet." Jesus answers him, "Unless I wash you, you have no part of me." Peter replies, in effect, "Well, in that case wash my whole body." Jesus says, "A person who has had a bath needs only to wash his feet; his whole body is clean." This is a picture of forgiveness. When we come to the cross we are made totally clean and we are forgiven—everything is dealt with. But as we go through the world we do things which tarnish our friendship with God. Our status is secure but our friendship is sullied with the dirt that we pick up on our feet as we go through life. Each day we need to pray, "Lord forgive us, cleanse us from the dirt." We don't need to have a bath again—Jesus has done that for us—but a measure of cleansing may be necessary every day.

Jesus went on to say, "If you forgive men when they sin against you, your heavenly Father will also forgive you. But if you do not forgive men their sins, your Father will not forgive your sins" (Matthew 6:14-15). This does not mean that by forgiving people we can earn forgiveness. We can never earn forgiveness. Jesus achieved that for us on the cross. But the sign that we are forgiven is that we are willing to forgive other people. If we are not willing to forgive other people that is evidence that we do not know forgiveness ourselves. If we really know God's forgiveness, we cannot refuse forgiveness to someone else.

"Lead us not into temptation, but deliver us from the evil one" (v. 13)

God does not tempt us (James 1:13), but He is in control of how much we are exposed to the devil (e.g., Job 1–2). Every Christian has a weak area—be it fear, selfish ambition, greed, pride, lust, gossiping, cynicism, or something else. If we know our weakness, we can pray for protection against it, and we can take action to avoid unnecessary temptation. We will consider this issue in chapter 11.

When should we pray?

The New Testament exhorts us to pray "always" (1 Thessalonians 5:17; Ephesians 6:18). We do not have to be in a special building in order to pray. We can pray on the train, on the bus, in the car, on our bike, walking along the road, as we lie in bed, in the middle of the night, whenever and wherever we are. As in any close relationship, we can chat as we do other things. Nevertheless, it is helpful to have time together when you know that you are meeting simply to talk. Jesus said, "When you pray, go into your room, close the door and pray to your Father, who is unseen" (Matthew 6:6). He Himself went off to a solitary place in order to pray (Mark 1:35). I find it helpful to combine Bible reading and prayer at the beginning of the day, when my mind is most active. It is good to have a regular pattern. What time of day we choose depends on many things including our characters, family life, and work patterns.

As well as praying alone, it is important to pray with other people. This could be in a small group of two or three for example. Jesus said, "I tell you that if two of you on earth agree about anything you ask for, it will be done for you by my Father in heaven" (Matthew 18:19). It can be very hard praying aloud in front of other people. I remember the first time I did this, about two months after I had come to Christ. I was with two of my closest friends and we decided that we would spend some time praying together. We only prayed for about ten minutes, but afterwards my shirt was wringing wet! Nevertheless, it is worth persevering since there is great power in praying together (Acts 12:5).

We were created by God to have a relationship with Him. Jesus' death on the cross made this possible and prayer is the way we deepen and strengthen our friendship with Him. That is why prayer is the most important activity of our lives.

CHAPTER 6

WHY AND HOW SHOULD I READ THE BIBLE?

My father had always wanted to visit Russia and when he was seventy-three and I was twenty-one we went on a family trip to the Soviet Union. At the time, Christians were being persecuted there and it was very hard to get hold of Bibles, but I took some Christian literature with me, including some Russian Bibles. While I was there I went to churches and looked for people who seemed to be genuine Christians. (At that time the meetings were often infiltrated by the KGB.)

On one occasion I followed a man, who was in his sixties, down the street after a service. Glancing round to check that nobody was there; I went up to him and tapped him on the shoulder. I took out one of my Bibles and handed it to him. For a moment he had an expression of disbelief. Then he took from his pocket a New Testament, which was probably 100 years old, the pages so threadbare they were virtually transparent. When he realized he had received a whole Bible, he was elated. He didn't speak any English, I didn't speak any Russian. We hugged each other and started dancing up and down the street jumping for joy—not something I normally do with someone I have never met or anyone else for that matter! That man knew that he had in his hands something truly unique.

Why was he so excited? Many today would see the Bible as rather dull, outdated, and irrelevant to their lives. Some prominent atheists go further and describe the God of the Bible as an "evil monster." Is this true? Is the Bible really something special? How is it unique?

First, it is uniquely popular. It is the world's best seller. It is estimated that a hundred million copies of the Bible are sold or given away every year and that there is an average of 6.8 Bibles in every American household. The Bible is the best selling book of all time—outselling all its rivals year in and year out, decade after decade. Gideon's International gives away a Bible every second. The Bible is available, in all or in part, in 2,426 languages.[38] An article in *The Times* was headlined "Forget the modern British novelists and TV tie-ins; the Bible is the biggest-selling book every year." The writer remarked:

> As usual the top seller by several miles was the ... Bible. If cumulative sales of the Bible were frankly reflected in bestseller lists, it would be a rare week when anything else would achieve a look in. It is wonderful, weird, or just plain baffling in this increasingly godless age—when the range of books available grows wider with each passing year—that this one book should go on selling hand over fist, month in, month out ... It is estimated that nearly 1.25 million Bibles and Testaments are sold in the U.K. each year.

The writer ends by saying, "*All* versions of the Bible sell well *all* the time. Can the Bible Society offer an explanation? I asked. 'Well,' I am told disarmingly, 'it is such a good book.'"

Second, it is uniquely powerful. As the former Prime Minister Stanley Baldwin said,

> The Bible is a high explosive. But it works in strange ways and no living man can tell or know how that book, in its journey through the world, has startled the individual soul in ten thousand different places into a new life, a new world, a new belief, a new conception, a new faith.[39]

When I read the Bible at university I was gripped by it. It came alive to me as it never had before and I couldn't put it down. This powerful encounter led to me putting my faith in Christ.

Third, it is uniquely precious. The psalmist says, "the words of God are more precious than gold." At her coronation the Queen was handed a Bible by the Moderator of the General Assembly of the Church of Scotland, with these words: "We present you with this book, the most valuable thing that this world affords."

Hugh Latimer, the sixteenth-century English bishop, once wrote that the books of the Bible should be constantly in our hands, in our eyes, in our ears, in our mouths, but most of all in our hearts. Scripture, he said, "turns our souls . . . it comforts, makes glad, cheers, and cherishes our conscience. It is a more excellent jewel or treasure than any gold or precious stone."[40]

Why is it so popular, so powerful, so precious? Jesus said: "Man does not live on bread alone, but on every word that comes from the mouth of God" (Matthew 4:4). The verb "comes" is in the present continuous tense, and means "is continually coming out of the mouth of God." God is continually wanting to communicate with His people and does so, primarily, through the Bible.

God has spoken: revelation

"In the past God spoke . . . at many times and in various ways, but in these last days he has spoken to us by his Son" (Hebrews 1:1-2). Christianity is a revealed faith. Jesus Christ is God's ultimate revelation.

The main way we know about Jesus is through God's revelation recorded in the Bible. Biblical theology should be the study of this revelation. God has also revealed Himself through creation (Romans 1:19-20; Psalm 19). Science is an exploration of God's revelation in creation. (There should be no conflict between science and the Christian faith; rather they complement one another.[41] Albert Einstein once said, "science without religion is lame, religion without science is blind . . . in truth a legitimate conflict between religion and science cannot exist."[42]) God also speaks to people directly by His Spirit: through prophecy, dreams, visions, and through other people. We will look at these in more detail later—especially in the chapter on guidance.

Paul wrote of the inspiration of the Scriptures that were available to him: "All Scripture is God-breathed and is useful for teaching, rebuking, correcting and training in righteousness, so that the man of God may be thoroughly equipped for every good work" (2 Timothy 3:16-17).

The Greek word for "God-breathed" is *theopneustos*. It is often translated as "inspired by God;" but literally it means "God-breathed." The writer is saying that Scripture is God speaking. Of course He used human authors. The Bible was written over a period of 1,500 years by at least forty authors, from a wide variety of backgrounds—kings, scholars, philosophers, fishermen, poets, statesmen, historians, and doctors. The Bible is 100 per cent the work of human beings, but it is also 100 per cent inspired by God (just as Jesus is fully human and fully God).

How can that be? This may be a puzzling paradox, but it is not a contradiction. Sir Christopher Wren, the greatest English architect of his time, built St. Paul's Cathedral. He started the project when he was forty-four, continuing the work for the next thirty-five years. It was completed in 1711 when he was seventy-nine. Wren built St. Paul's Cathedral, yet he never laid a single stone. There were many different builders but there was only one mind, one architect, and one inspiration. So it is with the Bible: there were many different writers but only one inspiration—God Himself.

It is clear from the Gospels that Jesus viewed the Scriptures as inspired by God. For Him, what the Scriptures said, God said (Mark 7:5-13). If Jesus is our Lord, our attitude to the Scriptures should be the same as His. "Belief in Christ as the supreme revelation of God leads to belief in scriptural inspiration—of the Old Testament by the direct testimony of Jesus and of the New Testament by inference from his testimony."[43]

This high view of the inspiration of the Bible has been held almost universally by the worldwide church down through the ages. The early theologians of the church had this view. Irenaeus (c. A.D. 130–200) said, "The Scriptures are perfect." Likewise, the reformers, for example, Martin Luther, spoke of "Scripture which has never erred." Today, the Roman Catholic official view is enshrined in Vatican II: the Scriptures "written under the inspiration of the Holy Spirit . . . have God as their author." Therefore, they must be acknowledged as being "without error."[44] This also, until the last century, was the view of all Protestant churches throughout the world, and although today it may be questioned and even ridiculed at a rudimentary level, it continues to be held by many fine scholars.

This does not mean that there are no difficulties in the Bible. Even Peter found some of Paul's letters "hard to understand" (2 Peter 3:16). There are moral and historical difficulties and some apparent contradictions. Some of the difficulties can be explained by the different contexts in which the many different authors were writing over such a substantial period of time. The Bible contains a whole range of literary genres: history, chronicle, narrative, poetry, prophecy, letters, wisdom, and apocalyptic literature.

Although some of the apparent contradictions can be explained by differing contexts, others are harder to resolve. This does not mean, however, that it is impossible or that we should abandon our belief in the inspiration of Scripture. Every great doctrine of the Christian faith should stretch our comprehension. For example, it is hard to reconcile the love of God and the suffering in the world. Yet every Christian believes in the love of God and seeks an understanding of the problem of suffering within that framework. I for one have found that as I have wrestled with this issue I have gained a greater understanding both of suffering and of the love of God.

In a similar way, it is important to hold on to the fact that *all* Scripture is inspired by God, even if we cannot immediately resolve every difficulty. If we do, it should transform the way in which we live our lives. When Billy Graham was a young man, several people (among them, there was one named Chuck) started to say to him, "You can't believe everything in the Bible." He began to worry about it and started to become very muddled. John Pollock, in his biography of the evangelist, records what happened:

> So I went back and I got my Bible, and I went out in the moonlight. And I got to a stump and put the Bible on the stump, and I knelt down, and I said, "Oh God; I cannot prove certain things. I cannot answer some of the questions Chuck is raising and some of the other people are raising, but I accept this Book by faith as the Word of God." I stayed by the stump praying wordlessly, my eyes moist . . . I had a tremendous sense of God's presence. I had a great peace that the decision I had made was right.[45]

If we accept that the Bible is inspired by God, then its authority must follow from that. If it is God's word, then it must be our supreme authority for what we believe and how we act. For Jesus, it was His supreme authority; above what the church leaders of His time said (e.g., Mark 7:1-20) and above the opinions of others, however clever they were (e.g., Mark 12:18-27). Having said that, we must of course give due weight to what church leaders and others say.

As we have seen, "All Scripture is God-breathed and is useful for teaching, rebuking, correcting and training in righteousness" (2 Timothy 3:16). First, it is our authority for what we believe—and therefore for "teaching." It's in the Bible that we find what God says (and what we should, therefore, believe) about suffering, about Jesus, about the cross and the resurrection and so on.

Secondly, it is our authority for how we act—for "rebuking," "correcting," and for "training in righteousness." It is here that we find out what is right and wrong in God's eyes—for example, the Ten Commandments have been described as "a brilliant analysis of the minimum conditions on which a society, a people, a nation can live a sober, righteous, and civilized life."[46]

There are some things that are very clear in the Bible. It tells us how to conduct our day-to-day lives. We find out what God thinks about relationships and family life. We know that the single state can be a high calling (1 Corinthians 7:7), but it is the exception rather than the rule; marriage is the norm (Genesis 2:24). We know that sexual intercourse outside marriage is wrong. We know that it is right to try to get a job if we can. We know that it is right to give and to forgive.

Some people say, "I don't want this rule book. It is too restrictive—all those rules and regulations. I want to be free. If you live by the Bible, you are not free to enjoy life." But is that really right? Does the Bible take away our freedom? Or does it in fact give us freedom? Rules and regulations can in fact create freedom and increase our enjoyment of life.

Some years ago, a soccer match had been arranged involving twenty-two small boys, including one of my sons, aged eight at the time. A friend of mine named Andy (who had been training the boys all year) was going to referee. Unfortunately, by 2:30 P.M. he had not shown up. The boys could wait no longer. I was pressured into being the substitute referee. There were a number of difficulties with this: I had no whistle; there were no markings for the boundaries; I didn't know any of the other boys' names; they did not have colors to distinguish which sides they were on; and I did not know the rules nearly as well as some of the boys.

The game soon descended into complete chaos. Some shouted that the ball was in. Others said that it was out. I wasn't at all sure, so I let things run. Then the fouls started. Some cried, "Foul!" Others said, "No foul!" I didn't know who was right. So I let them play on. Then people began to get hurt. By the time Andy arrived, there were three boys lying injured on the ground and all the rest were shouting, mainly at me! But the moment Andy arrived; he blew his whistle, arranged the teams, told them where the boundaries were, and had them under complete control. Then the boys had the game of their lives.

Were the boys more free without the rules or were they in fact less free? Without any effective authority they were free to do exactly what they wanted. The result was that people were confused and hurt. They much preferred it when they knew where the boundaries were. Then within those boundaries they were free to enjoy the game.

God has given us guidelines on how to live because He loves us and He wants us to enjoy life to the full. God did not say, "Do not murder," in order to ruin our enjoyment of life. Nor did He say "Do not commit adultery," because He is a spoilsport. He said these things because He did not want people to get hurt. The Bible is God's revelation of His will for all people. The more we live according to His will, the freer we shall be. God has spoken and we need to hear what He has said.

God speaks: relationship

For some people the Bible is never more than a well-thumbed manual for life. They analyze it, read commentaries on it (and there is nothing wrong with that), but we must remember that not only has God spoken, but He still speaks today through what He has said in the Bible. St. Gregory the Great said, "The Bible is a letter from God" and St. Augustine: "The Bible does nothing but speak of God's love for us."

For most of our married life my wife Pippa and I haven't had to be apart for substantial periods of time. But I remember I once had to be away for three and a half weeks. Each morning at the place I was staying I would rush down and check the hall table for any letters. If I saw her handwriting my heart would leap. Why? Because it was a letter from the person I loved. Similarly the Bible is God's love letter to us.

The main point of the Bible is to show us how to enter into a relationship with God through Jesus Christ. Jesus said, "You diligently study the Scriptures because you think that by them you possess eternal life. These are the Scriptures that testify about me, yet you refuse to come to me to have life" (John 5:39-40).

To use an analogy, imagine for a moment that I drive an aging Nissan. This car has served me well and being pleased with it I decide to order a brand new Nissan to be delivered to my home. When it arrives at our front door I go outside and admire it. As I check out the inside of the car, I discover in the glove compartment the Nissan manual. Excited by this find I take the manual inside and start studying it. I then get out my felt-tip pen and begin to underline sections that I like and then to learn them by heart. I also cut out some sections and stick them to my bathroom mirror so that I can read them while shaving. I even join a club of like-minded manual enthusiasts. There they encourage me to learn Japanese, so that I can study the manual in its original language. Remember this is an analogy! If this were true clearly I would have missed the point; the purpose of the manual is to help us to drive the car. In the same way, it is no good studying the Bible if we miss the point, which is to come into a living relationship with Jesus. Martin Luther said, "Scripture is the manger or 'cradle' in which the infant Jesus lies. Don't let us inspect the cradle and forget to worship the baby."

Our relationship with God is two-way. We speak to Him in prayer and He speaks to us in many ways, but especially through the Bible. God speaks through what He has spoken. The writer of the Epistle to the Hebrews says when He quotes the Old Testament, "As the Holy Spirit *says*" (Hebrews 3:7). It is not just that the Holy Spirit spoke in the past. He still speaks through what He said in the Bible. This is what makes the Bible so alive. Again, as Martin Luther put it, "The Bible is alive, it speaks to me; it has feet, it runs after me; it has hands, it lays hold on me."

What happens when God speaks?

First, He brings faith to those who are not yet Christians. Paul says, "Faith comes from hearing the message, and the message is heard through the word of Christ" (Romans 10:17). It is often as people read the Bible that they come to faith in Jesus Christ. That was certainly my experience and it has been the experience of many other people.

Actor David Suchet, well-known for his title role in *Poirot*, tells how a few years ago he was lying in his bath in a hotel in the United States, when he had a sudden and impulsive desire to read the Bible.

He managed to find a Gideon Bible and he started to read the New Testament. As he read, he came to put his faith in Jesus Christ. He said:

> From somewhere I got this desire to read the Bible again. That's the most important part of my conversion. I started with the Acts of the Apostles and then moved to Paul's Letters—Romans and Corinthians. And it was only after that I came to the gospels. In the New Testament I suddenly discovered the way that life should be followed.

Second, He speaks to Christians. As we read the Bible we experience a transforming relationship with God through Jesus Christ. Paul says, "We, who with unveiled faces all reflect the Lord's glory, are being transformed into his likeness with ever-increasing glory, which comes from the Lord, who is the Spirit" (2 Corinthians 3:18). As we study the Bible, we come into contact with Jesus Christ. It has always struck me as the most extraordinarily wonderful fact that we can speak to and hear from the person whom we read about in the pages of the New Testament—the same Jesus Christ. He will speak to us (not audibly, on the whole, but in our heart) as we read the Bible. We will hear His message for us. As we spend time with Him, our characters will become more like His.

Spending time in His presence, listening to His voice, brings many blessings. He often brings joy and peace, even in the middle of a crisis in our lives (Psalm 23:5). When we are not sure which direction we should be going in, God often guides us through His Word (Psalm 119:105). The Book of Proverbs even tells us that God's words bring healing to our bodies (Proverbs 4:22).

The Bible also provides us with a defense against spiritual attack. We only have one detailed example of Jesus facing temptation. Jesus faced intense attack by the devil at the start of His ministry (Matthew 4:1-11). Jesus met every temptation with a verse from the Scriptures. I find it fascinating that every one of His replies came from Deuteronomy 6–8. It seems plausible to infer that Jesus had been studying this portion of Scripture and that it was fresh in His mind.

The Word of God has great power. The writer of the Book of Hebrews says, "The word of God is living and active. Sharper than any double-edged sword, it penetrates even to dividing soul and spirit, joints and marrow; it judges the thoughts and attitudes of the heart" (Hebrews 4:12). It has power to pierce all our defenses and get through to our hearts. I remember once reading Philippians 2:4, "Each of you should look not only to your own interests, but also to the interests of others." It was like an arrow going straight into me as I realized how selfish I was being. In these, and many other ways, God's Word speaks to us.

As God speaks to us and we learn to hear His voice, our relationship with Him grows, and our love for Him deepens. Rick Warren has written that reading the Bible, "generates life, creates faith, produces change . . . heals hurts, builds character, transforms circumstances, imparts joy, overcomes adversity, defeats temptation, infuses hope, releases power [and] cleanses our minds."[47]

How do we hear God speak through the Bible?

Time is our most valuable possession. The pressure on time tends to increase as life goes on and we become busier and busier. There is a saying that goes "money is power, but time is life." If we are going to set aside time to read the Bible, we have to plan ahead. If we don't plan we will never do it. Don't be depressed if you only keep to 80 per cent of your plan. Sometimes we oversleep!

It is wise to start with a realistic goal. Don't be over-ambitious. It is better to spend a few minutes every day than to spend an hour-and-a-half the first day and then to give up. If you have never studied the Bible before, you might like to set aside seven minutes every day. I am sure that if you do that regularly you will steadily increase it.

Mark tells us that Jesus got up early and went off to a *solitary place* to pray (Mark 1:35). It is important to try to find some place where we can be on our own. I find that first thing in the morning is the best time. I take a cup of coffee, the Bible, my appointment calendar, and a notebook. I use the notebook to write down prayers and also things I think God may be saying to me. I use the calendar to help me pray about each stage of my day, but also for jotting down any distracting thoughts or plans that come to my mind.

I start by asking God to speak to me through the passage I am reading. Then I read it. It's a good idea to start by reading a few verses of one of the Gospels each day. You might find it helpful to use Bible reading notes, [48] which are available at most Christian bookshops, or perhaps a Bible study website.

As I read, I ask myself three questions:

1. *What does it say?* I read it at least once and, if necessary, compare different translations.

2. *What does it mean?* What did it mean to the person who first wrote it and those who first read it? (This is where the notes may be helpful.)

3. *How does it apply to me, my family, my work, my neighbors, and the society around me?* (It is when we see the relevance to our own lives that Bible reading becomes so exciting and we become conscious that we are hearing God's voice.)

Finally, we must put into practice what we hear from God. Jesus said, "Therefore everyone who hears these words of mine and puts them into practice is like a wise man who built his house on the rock" (Matthew 7:24). As D. L. Moody pointed out, "The Bible was not given to increase our knowledge. It was given to change lives."

I would encourage you to develop a regular pattern of reading the Bible each day and praying that God would speak to you. It is an amazing experience when He does. Sometimes reading the Bible can be mundane, but sometimes it is particularly significant. This has certainly been my experience. God spoke to me very clearly about my father after he died in 1981. I had become a Christian seven years earlier and my parents' initial reaction was one of complete horror. Gradually, over the years, they began to see a change in me. My mother became a committed Christian long before she died. My father was a man of few words. Initially, he was very unsure about my involvement in the Christian faith. By degrees, he started to become warmer about it. His death was quite sudden. I missed him dreadfully but what I found hardest about his death was that I wasn't sure whether he was a Christian or not.

Exactly ten days after his death, I was reading the Bible. I had asked God to speak to me about my father that day because I was still worrying about him. I happened to be reading Romans and I came across the verse, "Everyone who calls on the name of the Lord will be saved" (Romans 10:13). I sensed at that moment God was saying to me that this verse was for my father; that he had called on the name of the Lord and been "saved." About five minutes later my wife, Pippa, came in and said to me, "I have been reading a verse in Acts 2:21 and I think this verse is for your father. It says, '. . . and everyone who calls on the name of the Lord will be saved.'" It was quite extraordinary because that verse only appears twice in the New Testament and God had spoken to both of us through the same words at the same time in different parts of the Bible.

Three days later, we went to a Bible study in a friend's home and the Bible study was on Romans 10:13, that same passage. So three times during those three days God spoke to me about my father through the same words. Nevertheless, on my way to work I was still thinking about my father and worrying about him. As I came out of the subway, I looked up and there was a huge poster saying, "Whoever calls upon the name of the Lord will be saved" (Romans 10:13). I remember talking to a friend about it and telling him what had happened. He said to me, "Do you think the Lord may be trying to speak to you?"

CHAPTER 7

HOW DOES GOD GUIDE US?

We all have to make decisions in life. We are faced with decisions about relationships, marriage, children, use of time, jobs, homes, money, holidays, possessions, giving, and so on. Some of these are big decisions; some are smaller. In many cases, it is of the utmost importance that we make the right decisions—for instance in our choice of a marriage partner. We need God's help.

One wonderful thing that the Christian faith shows us is that we are not on our own in this life. Guidance springs out of our relationship with God. He promises to guide those who are walking with Him. He says: "I will instruct you and teach you in the way you should go" (Psalm 32:8). Jesus promises to lead and guide His followers, "He calls his own sheep by name and leads them out . . . his sheep follow him because they know his voice" (John 10:3-4). Jesus uses the analogy of a sheep with his shepherd to talk about the relationship that He wants to have with us. He longs for us to discover His will (Colossians 1:9; Ephesians 5:17). He is concerned for each of us as individuals. He loves us and wants to speak to us about what we should be doing with our lives—about little things as well as big things.

God has a plan for our lives (Ephesians 2:10). Sometimes people are worried by this. They think, "I'm not sure that I want God's plan for my life. Will His plans be good?" We need not fear. God loves us and wants the very best for our lives. Paul tells us that God's will for our lives is "good, pleasing and perfect" (Romans 12:2). He said to His people through the prophet Jeremiah: "'For I know the plans I have for you,' declares the Lord, 'plans to prosper you and not to harm you, plans to give you hope and a future'"(Jeremiah 29:11). He is saying,

"Don't you realize that I have a really good plan for your life? I have prepared something wonderful." This cry from God's heart came because He saw the mess His people had gotten themselves into when they didn't follow His plans. All around us we see people whose lives are in a muddle. After they have come to Christ people often say to me, "I wish I had become a Christian five or ten years earlier. Look at my life now. It is such a mess."

If we are to find out about God's plans for us, we need to ask Him about them. God warned His people about embarking on plans without consulting Him: "'Woe to the obstinate children,' declares the Lord, 'to those who carry out plans that are not mine . . . who go down to Egypt *without consulting me*'"(Isaiah 30:1-2, italics mine). Of course, Jesus is the supreme example of doing the will of His Father. He was consistently "led by the Spirit" (Luke 4:1) and only did what He saw His Father doing (John 5:19).

Sometimes we make mistakes because we fail to consult God. We make a plan and think, "I want to do that but I am not quite sure whether God wants me to do it. I think I'd better not ask Him, just in case it's not His will for me!"

God guides us when we are prepared to do His will rather than insisting that our own way is right. The psalmist says, "He guides the humble" (Psalm 25:9) and "confides in those who fear [respect] him" (v. 14). God guides those whose attitude is like Mary's: "I am the Lord's servant and I am willing to do whatever he wants" (Luke 1:38, *The Living Bible*). The moment we are prepared to do His will, He begins to reveal His plans for our lives.

There is a verse in the Psalms, which I go back to time and time again: "Commit your way to the Lord; trust in him, and he will act" (Psalm 37:5, RSV). Our part is to commit the decision to the Lord and then to trust Him. When we have done that, we can wait expectantly for Him to act.

Towards the end of our time in college, a friend of mine named Nicky, who had become a Christian about the same time that I did, become very close to a girl who was not a Christian. He felt it was not right to marry her unless she shared his faith in Christ. He did not want to put her under any pressure. So he did what the psalmist said and committed it to the Lord. He said, in effect, "Lord, if this relationship is not right, I pray that you will stop it. If it is right, then I pray she will become a Christian by the last day of the spring semester." He did not tell her, or anyone else, about this date. He put his "trust in Him" and waited for God to act. The final day of the spring semester arrived and they happened to be going to a party together that night. Just before midnight, she told him she wanted to go for a drive. So they got into the car and she gave him a whole string of directions off the top of her head, just for fun: "Three left turns, three right turns, drive straight for three miles and stop." He played along and followed them. They ended up in the American cemetery, which has one enormous cross in the center, surrounded by hundreds of little crosses. She was shocked and deeply moved by the symbol of the cross, and also by the fact that God had used her instructions to get her attention. She burst into tears. Moments later, she came to faith in Christ. They have now been happily married for many years and still look back and remember how God's hand was on them at that moment.

Given that we are willing to do what God wants us to do, in what ways should we expect God to speak to us and guide us? There are various ways in which He guides us. Sometimes God speaks through one of the ways set out below; sometimes it is a combination. If it is a major decision, He may speak through all of them. They are sometimes called the five "C Ss."

Commanding Scripture

As we have seen, God's general will for all people in all places and all circumstances is revealed in Scripture. In the Bible God has told us what He thinks about a whole range of issues. We know from the Bible that certain things are wrong. We can therefore be quite sure that God will not guide us to do these things. Sometimes a married person says, "I have fallen in love with this man/woman. We love each other so much. I feel God is leading me to leave my husband/wife and to start this new relationship." But God has already made His will clear. He has said, "You shall not commit adultery" (Exodus 20:14).

Sometimes people feel led to save money by not paying their income tax. But God has made it clear that we are to pay any taxes that are due (Romans 13:7). I came across a letter that was written to the Inland Revenue by a man who had just become a Christian. He wrote:

"Dear Sir, I have just become a Christian and have found that I cannot sleep at night. So here is a hundred pounds that I owe you. P.S. If I still can't sleep, I'll send you the rest."

God also calls us to be people of integrity and tell the truth (Exodus 20:16). I remember once meeting an old man whose nickname was Gibbo. Many years before, he had worked as a clerk in Selfridges, the famous London department store. His boss was the founder, Gordon Selfridge. One day the phone rang; Gibbo picked it up and the caller asked to speak to Gordon Selfridge. Selfridge was in the room, but when Gibbo motioned to him, he said, "Tell him I'm out." Gibbo handed him the phone and said, "You tell him you're out!" After he put the phone down, Selfridge was furious. But Gibbo stood his ground and said to him, "If I can lie for you, I can lie to you and I never will." This action transformed Gibbo's career at Selfridges. From that moment on, when his employers needed someone they could really trust, they turned to him. He had proved his integrity.

In these, and many other areas, God has revealed His general will. We do not need to ask for His guidance because He has already given it. If we are not sure, we may need to ask someone who knows the Bible better than we do whether there is anything addressing that issue. Once we have discovered what the Bible says, we need search no further.

Although God's general will is revealed in the Bible, we cannot always find His particular will for our lives there. It does not tell us which job we should do, how much money we should give away, or whom we should marry.

As we saw in the chapter on the Bible, God still speaks through the Scriptures today. He may speak to us as we read. The psalmist says, "Your statutes . . . are my counselors" (Psalm 119:24). That is not to say that we find God's will by opening the Bible at random and seeing what it says. Rather, if we get into a regular Bible reading habit, sometimes it can be quite extraordinary how appropriate each day's reading seems to be for our own particular circumstances.

Sometimes a verse seems almost to leap off the page at us and we sense God speaking through it. This was certainly my experience when I sensed God calling me to change jobs. The choice I faced was between carrying on with law or becoming a vicar. Each time I felt God speaking to me as I read the Bible, I wrote it down. On one occasion, for example, when I had been praying to God to guide me, I read the verse, "How can they believe in the one of whom they have not heard? And how can they hear without someone preaching to them?" (Romans 10:14). This happened on a Thursday. I then drove to Durham for the weekend to see some friends and pray about the decision I had to make. Out of the blue, my friend read out that verse. I was amazed! On the Sunday evening, I was at church back in London. At the beginning of the service the speaker announced, not only that he was to be preaching on this same verse but, that through it he felt God was calling somebody to ordination in the Church of England. I noted at least fifteen different occasions in which I believe God spoke to me through the Bible about this call.

Compelling Spirit

Guidance is very personal. When we become Christians, the Spirit of God comes to live within us. When He does so, He begins to communicate with us. We need to learn to hear His voice. Jesus said that His sheep (His followers) would recognize His voice (John 10:4-5). We recognize a good friend's voice immediately on the phone. If we do not know the person so well, it may be harder and take more time. The more we get to know Jesus, the easier we will find it to recognize His voice.

St. Paul says, "And now, compelled by the Spirit, I'm going to Jerusalem." Paul's expectation was that all Christians were led by the Spirit (Galatians 5:18). On another occasion, we find Paul and his companions planning to enter Bithynia, "but the Spirit of Jesus would not allow them to" (Acts 16:7). So they went a different way. We do not know exactly how the Spirit spoke to them, but it may have been in one of a number of ways.

Here are three examples of ways in which God speaks by His Spirit.

1. God often speaks to us as we pray

In Acts 13, we read that "as they were worshiping the Lord, the Holy Spirit spoke to them." Prayer is a two-way conversation. Suppose I go to the doctor and say, "Doctor, I have a number of problems: I have fungus growing under my toenails, my eyes itch, I need a flu shot, I have very bad backaches, and I have tennis elbow." Then, having gone through my list of complaints, I look at my watch and say, "Goodness me, time is getting away. Well, I must be going. Thanks very much for listening." The doctor might want to say, "Hang on a second. Do you not want to hear what I have to say?" If, whenever we pray, we only speak to God and never take time to listen, we make the same mistake. It's for this reason that I have a notebook next to me when I pray. I find it helpful to jot down thoughts that come into my mind like, "perhaps I should call or write to that person."

In the Bible we find God speaking to His people. For example, on one occasion as the Christians "were worshiping the Lord and fasting, the Holy Spirit said, 'Set apart for me Barnabas and Saul for the work to which I have called them.' So after they had fasted and prayed, they placed their hands on them and sent them off" (Acts 13:2-3).

Again, we don't know exactly how the Holy Spirit spoke. It may be that as they were praying the thought came into their minds. That is a common way in which God speaks. People sometimes describe it as "impressions" or "knowing it deep down." It is possible for the Holy Spirit to speak in all of these ways.

Obviously such thoughts and feelings need to be tested (1 John 4:1). Is the impression in line with the Bible? Does it promote love? If it does not, it cannot come from a God who is love (1 John 4:16). Is it strengthening, encouraging, and comforting (1 Corinthians 14:3)? When we have made the decision, do we know God's peace (Colossians 3:15)?

2. God sometimes speaks to us by giving us a strong desire to do something

"God . . . works in you to *will* and to act according to his good purpose" (Philippians 2:13, italics mine). As we surrender our wills to God, He works in us and often changes our desires.

A young British doctor named Paul Brand was once visiting a leprosy sanatorium near Chennai (formerly Madras), India. As he was being shown around the hospital by a man named Dr. Cochrane, he saw patients who were squatting and stumping along on bandaged feet, following the two doctors with their unseeing, deformed faces.

Dr. Brand said this:

> Hands waved at me and stretched out in greeting ... They were twisted, gnarled, ulcerated stumps. Some were stiff like metal claws. Some were missing fingers. Some hands were missing altogether. Finally I could restrain myself no longer. "How did they get this way? What do you do about them?" [Dr. Cochrane said,] "I don't know ... I am a skin man—I can treat that part of the leprosy. But you are a bone man, the orthopedic surgeon!" ... He went on to tell me that not one orthopedic surgeon had yet studied the deformities of the fifteen million leprosy victims in the world.

As they were passing, a young person who had leprosy put out his hand, and Paul Brand said to him, "Squeeze my hand as hard as you can." He has said of that encounter:

> To my amazement instead of the twitch I'd expected to feel, this sharp and intense pain raced through my palm. His grip was like a vice, with fingers digging into my flesh like steel talons. He showed no paralysis—in fact, I cried out for him to let go. I looked up angrily, but was alarmed by the gentle smile on his face. He didn't know he was hurting me. That was the clue: somewhere in that severely deformed hand were powerfully good muscles. I felt a tingling, as if the whole universe was revolving around me. I knew I had arrived in my place. That single incident in 1947 changed my life. It was my moment. I'd felt a call of the Spirit of God. I was made for that one moment, and knew that I would have to point my life in a new direction. I've never doubted it since.[49]

Dr. Brand went on to discover that leprosy destroyed the sensation of pain in affected parts of the body, so patients inadvertently injured and destroyed themselves. This was entirely due to infection, and thus preventable. This led to pioneering research into the disease, and Dr. Brand became a world-renowned leprosy surgeon, receiving a CBE and the Albert Lasker award.

3. God sometimes guides in more unusual ways

There are many examples in the Bible of God guiding individuals in dramatic ways. When Samuel was a small boy, God spoke to him in such a way that he was able to physically hear God's words with his own ears (1 Samuel 3:4-14). He guided Abraham (Genesis 18), Joseph (Matthew 2:19) and Peter (Acts 12:7) through angels. In both the Old Testament and the New Testament (e.g., Agabus—Acts 11:27-28; 21:10-11), God often spoke through prophets. He guided through visions (sometimes referred to today as "pictures"). For example, one night God spoke to Paul in a vision. He saw a man in Macedonia standing and begging him, "Come over to Macedonia and help us." Not surprisingly, Paul and his companions took this as guidance that God had called them to preach the gospel in Macedonia (Acts 16:10).

We also find examples of God guiding through dreams (e.g., Matthew 1:20; 2:12-13, 22). I was praying for a couple who were good friends of ours. The husband had recently come to faith in Christ. The wife was highly intelligent, but strongly against what had happened to her husband. She became a little hostile towards us. One night I had a dream in which I saw her face quite changed, her eyes full of the joy of the Lord. This encouraged us to continue praying and keeping close to both of them. A few months later she came to faith in Christ. I remember looking at her and seeing the face I had seen in the dream a few months earlier.

These are all ways in which God has guided people in the past, and how He still does today.

Common sense

When we become Christians, we are not called to abandon common sense. The New Testament writers often encourage us to think and never discourage us from using our minds (e.g., 2 Timothy 2:7).

If we abandon common sense, then we get ourselves into absurd situations. In his book *Knowing God*, J. I. Packer quotes an example of a woman who each morning, having consecrated the day to the Lord as soon as she woke, "would then ask him whether she was to get up or not," and would not stir till "the voice" told her to dress.

> As she put on each article she asked the Lord whether she was to put it on and very often the Lord would tell her to put on the right shoe and leave off the other; sometimes she was to put on both stockings and no

> shoes; and sometimes both shoes and no stockings. It was the same with all the articles of dress ...[50]

It is true to say that God's promises of guidance were not given so that we could avoid the strain of thinking. Indeed, John Wesley, the father of Methodism, said that God usually guided him by presenting reasons to his mind for acting in a certain way. This is important in every area, both in the ordinary day-to-day decisions of life, but also concerning marriage and jobs. Common sense is one of the factors to be taken into account in the whole area of choosing a marriage partner for life. It is common sense to consider at least three important aspects.

First, are we *spiritually compatible*? Paul warns of the danger of marrying someone who is not a Christian (2 Corinthians 6:14). In practice, if one of the parties is not a Christian, it nearly always leads to a great tension in the marriage. This happens because the two people are going in different directions. The Christian feels torn between the desire to serve their spouse and their desire to serve the Lord. However, spiritual compatibility means more than the fact that both are Christians. It means that each party respects the other's faith, rather than simply being able to say, "At least they pass the test of being a Christian."

Secondly, are we *personally compatible*? Obviously, our spouse should be a very good friend and someone with whom we have a great deal in common. One of the many advantages of not sleeping together before getting married is that it is easier to concentrate on the area of personal compatibility. Often the sexual side can dominate the early stages of a relationship. If the foundations have not been built on friendship then, when the initial sexual excitement wears off, it can leave the relationship without a solid base.

Third, are we *physically compatible*? By this I mean that we should be attracted to each other. It is not enough to be spiritually and emotionally compatible. Often people put sexual compatibility first, but this comes last in the order of priorities. Is it necessary to sleep together in order to see whether there is sexual compatibility? No, this approach raises the question, how many sexual encounters do we need before we can make a rationally informed choice?

Again, common sense is vital when considering God's guidance about our jobs and careers. Sometimes people say, "I've become a Christian. Should I leave my job?' The answer is given by Paul: ". . . retain the place in life that the Lord has assigned to [you] and to which God has called [you]" (1 Corinthians 7:17). Unless our job is

totally incompatible with the Christian faith, St. Paul is telling us to live out the Christian life in whatever setting that call took place.

The general rule is that we should stay in our current job (if we are employed) until God calls us to do something else. God does not tend to call us *out of* things, rather he calls us *into* things. To discern what God might be calling us into, we should ask ourselves, "What is my temperament? What is my personality? What am I good at? What do I like doing? What are my gifts?" It is also common sense to take a long-term view of life. It is wise to look ahead ten, fifteen, twenty years and ask the questions: "Where is my present job taking me? Is that where I want to go in the long term? Or is my long-term vision for something quite different? In which case, where should I be now in order to get there?"

Counsel of the saints

The word "saints" is used in the New Testament to mean "all Christians"—in other words, the church (e.g., Philippians 1:1). It is wonderful to be part of a community of Christians, in which we can help one another in making our decisions. We need to have the humility to recognize that God does not just speak to "me," but that He also speaks to other people, and He has done so through history.

The Book of Proverbs is full of injunctions to seek wise advice. The writer asserts that "the wise listen to advice" (Proverbs 12:15). He warns that "plans fail for lack of counsel," but on the other hand, "with many advisers they succeed" (Proverbs 15:22). Therefore, he urges, "make plans by seeking advice" (Proverbs 20:18).

While seeking advice is very important, we need to remember that, ultimately, our decisions are between us and God. They are our responsibility. We cannot shift that responsibility onto others or seek to blame them if things go wrong. The "counsel of the saints" is part of guidance—but it is not the only part. Sometimes it may be right to go ahead in spite of the advice of others.

If we are faced with a decision and we need advice, whom should we consult? To the writer of the Proverbs, "The fear of the Lord is the beginning of wisdom . . ." (Proverbs 9:10). Probably, therefore, he is thinking of advice from those who fear or respect the Lord. The best advisers are often people whom we respect; they are usually godly Christian people with wisdom and experience. It may also be wise to seek the advice of our parents, even if we no longer live at home. They probably know us better than anyone else, and in asking them we honor them (Exodus 20:12).

I have found it a real help throughout my Christian life to have someone to whom I can go for advice on a whole range of issues: a mature Christian whom I respect. At different times I have turned to different people. I am so grateful to God for their wisdom and help in many areas. Often God's insight came as we talked through the issues together.

When it comes to bigger decisions, I have found it helpful to seek a range of advice. Over the question of ordination, I sought the advice of two such men, my two closest friends, my vicar, and those who were involved in the official process of selection.

The people whom we ask for advice should not be chosen on the basis that they will agree with what we have already planned to do! Sometimes one sees a person consulting countless people in the hope that they will eventually find somebody who will endorse their plans.

Such advice has little weight and simply enables the person to say, "I consulted x and he or she agreed." We should consult people on the basis of their spiritual authority, or their relationship to us, regardless of what we may anticipate their views to be.

Circumstantial signs

God is in ultimate control of all events. The writer of Proverbs points out: "In his heart a man plans his course, but the Lord determines his steps" (Proverbs 16:9). Sometimes God opens doors (1 Corinthians 16:9) and sometimes He closes them (Acts 16:7). There have been two occasions in my life when God has closed the door on something I very much wanted, and which I believed at the time was God's will. I tried to force the doors open. I prayed and I struggled and I fought, but they would not open. On both occasions I was bitterly disappointed. But I understand now, years later, why He closed those doors. Indeed I am grateful that He did. However, I am not sure I will ever know, this side of heaven, why God has closed certain doors in my life.

Sometimes He opens doors in a remarkable way. The circumstances and the timing point clearly to the hand of God (e.g., Genesis 24). Michael Bourdeaux is the founder and president of Keston College, a research unit devoted to helping Christians in what were communist lands. His work and research are respected by governments all over the world. He studied Russian at Oxford and his Russian teacher, Dr. Zernov, sent him a letter that he had received because he thought it would interest him. It detailed how monks were being beaten up by the KGB and subjected to inhuman medical examinations and how they were being rounded up in trucks and dumped many hundreds of miles away. The letter was written very simply, with no adornment, and as he read it Michael Bourdeaux felt he was hearing the true voice of the persecuted church. The letter was signed "Varavva and Pronina."

In August 1964, he went on a trip to Moscow and on his first evening there met up with old friends who explained that the persecutions were getting worse; in particular, the old church of St. Peter and St. Paul had been demolished. They suggested that he go to see it for himself.

So he took a taxi, arriving at dusk. When he came to the square where he had remembered a very beautiful church, he found nothing except a twelve-foot-high fence which hid the rubble where the church had been. Over on the other side of the square, climbing the fence to try to see what was inside, were two women. He watched them, and when they finally left the square he followed them for a hundred yards and eventually caught up with them. They asked, "Who are you?" He replied, "I am a foreigner. I have come to find out what is happening here in the Soviet Union."

They took him back to the house of another woman, who asked him why he had come. He said he had received a letter from the Ukraine via Paris. When she asked who it was from, he replied, "Varavva and Pronina." There was silence. He wondered if he had said something wrong. There followed a flood of uncontrolled sobbing. The woman pointed and said, "This is Varavva, and this is Pronina."

The population of Russia is over 140 million. The Ukraine, from where the letter was written, is 1,300 kilometers from Moscow. Michael Bourdeaux had flown from England six months after the letter had been written. They would not have met had either party arrived at the demolished church an hour earlier or an hour later. That was one of the ways in which God called Michael Bourdeaux to set up his life's work, Keston College.[51]

Sometimes God's guidance seems to come as soon as it is asked for (e.g., Genesis 24), but often it takes much longer; sometimes months or even years. We may have a sense that God is going to do something in our lives, but have to wait a long time for it to happen. On these occasions we need patience like that of Abraham who "after waiting patiently . . . received what was promised" (Hebrews 6:15). He spent most of his life waiting for God to fulfill a promise He had given him when he was a young man, which was not fulfilled until he was an old man. While waiting, he was tempted at one point to try and force the issue, to fulfill God's promises by his own means—with disastrous results (see Genesis 16 and 21).

Sometimes we hear God correctly, but we get the timing wrong. God spoke to Joseph in a dream about what would happen to him and his family. He probably expected immediate fulfillment, but he had to wait years. Indeed, while he was in prison it must have been hard for him to believe that his dreams would ever be fulfilled. But thirteen years after the original dream, he saw God's fulfillment. The waiting was part of the preparation (see Genesis 37–50).

In this area of guidance, we all make mistakes. Sometimes, like Abraham, we try to fulfill God's purpose by our own wrong methods. Like Joseph, we get the timing wrong. Sometimes we feel that we have made too much of a mess of our lives by the time we come to Christ for God to do anything with us. But God is greater than that. Oscar Wilde, author and playwright, said, "Every saint has a past, and every sinner has a future."[52] God is able to "restore to you the years which the swarming locust has eaten" (Joel 2:25, RSV). He is able to make something good out of whatever is left of our lives—whether it is a short time or a long time—if we will offer what we have to Him and co-operate with His Spirit.

Lord Radstock was staying in a hotel in Norway in the mid-nineteenth century. He heard a little girl playing the piano down in

the hallway. She was making a terrible noise: "Plink . . . plonk . . . plink . . ." It was driving him crazy! A man came and sat beside her and began playing alongside her, filling in the gaps. The result was the most beautiful music. He later discovered that the man playing alongside was the girl's father, Alexander Borodin, composer of the opera *Prince Igor*.

Paul writes that "in all things God works for the good of those who love him, who have been called according to his purpose" (Romans 8:28). As we falteringly play our part—seeking His will for our lives by reading (commanding Scripture), listening (compelling Spirit), thinking (common sense), talking (counsel of the saints), watching (circumstantial signs) and waiting—God comes and sits alongside us "and in all things . . . works for the good." He takes our "plink . . . plonk . . . plonk . . ." and makes something beautiful out of our lives.

CHAPTER 8

WHO IS THE HOLY SPIRIT?

I had a group of friends at university, five of whom were named Nicky! We used to meet for lunch most days. In February 1974, most of us came to faith in Jesus Christ. We immediately became very enthusiastic about our new-found faith. One of the Nickys, however, was slow to get going. He didn't seem excited about his relationship with God, with reading the Bible, or with praying.

One day, someone prayed for him to be filled with the Spirit and it transformed his life. A great big smile came across his face. He became well known for his radiance—and he still is, years later. From then on, if there was a Bible study, a prayer meeting, or a church in reach, Nicky was there. He loved to be with other Christians. He became the most magnetic personality. People were drawn to him and he helped many others to believe and to be filled with the Spirit in the way that he had been.

What was it that made such a difference to Nicky? I think that he would answer that it was his experience of the Holy Spirit. Many people know a certain amount about God the Father and Jesus the Son. But there is a great deal of ignorance about the Holy Spirit. Hence, three chapters of this book are devoted to the third person of the Trinity.

Some old translations speak of the "Holy Ghost" and this can make Him seem a little frightening.[53] As an old limerick puts it:

There was a young man who said, "Run!
The end of the world has begun!
It's that old Holy Ghost

I'm frightened of most
I can manage the Father and Son!"

The Holy Spirit is not a ghost, but a person. He has all the characteristics of personhood. He thinks (Acts 15:28), speaks (Acts 1:16), leads (Romans 8:14) and can be grieved (Ephesians 4:30). He is sometimes described as the Spirit of Christ (Romans 8:9) or the Spirit of Jesus (Acts 16:7). He is the way in which Jesus is present with His people.

What is He like? He is sometimes described in the original Greek as the *parakletos* (John 14:16). This is a difficult word to translate. It means "one called alongside"—a counselor, a comforter, and an encourager. Jesus said the Father will give you "another" counselor. The word for "another" here implies "another of the same kind." In other words, the Holy Spirit is just like Jesus.

In this chapter, I want to look at the person of the Holy Spirit: who He is and what we can learn about Him as we trace His activity through the Bible from Genesis 1 right through to the Day of Pentecost. Because the Pentecostal movement began about a hundred years ago, it might be tempting to think that the Holy Spirit is a relatively new phenomenon. This is, of course, far from the truth.

He was involved in creation

We see evidence of the activity of the Holy Spirit in the opening verses of the Bible: "In the beginning God created the heavens and the earth. Now the earth was formless and empty, darkness was over the surface of the deep, and the Spirit of God was hovering over the waters" (Genesis 1:1-2). Like a bird hovering over her nest, waiting, the Holy Spirit was about to bring something new into being. The whole Trinity was involved in creation (John 1:3).

We see in the account of the creation how the Spirit of God caused new things to come into being and brought order out of chaos. He is the same Spirit today. He often brings new things into people's lives and into churches. He brings order and peace into chaotic lives, freeing people from addictions and from the confusion and mess of broken relationships.

When God created human beings, He "formed the man from the dust of the ground and breathed into his nostrils the breath of life, and the man became a living being" (Genesis 2:7). The Hebrew word implied for breath here is *ruach*, which is also the word for "Spirit." The *ruach* of God brings physical life to humanity formed from dust. Likewise, He brings spiritual life to people and churches, both of which can be as dry as dust.

Some years ago I was speaking to a clergyman who was telling me that his life and his church had been like that—a bit dusty. One day, however, he and his wife were filled with the Spirit of God. They found a new enthusiasm for the Bible, and their lives were transformed. His church became a center of life. The youth group, started by his son who had also been filled with the Spirit, experienced explosive growth and became one of the largest in the area.

Many are hungry for life and are attracted to people and churches where they see the life of the Spirit of God.

He came upon particular people at particular times for particular tasks

When the Spirit of God comes upon people something happens. He does not just evoke a feeling of inner peace. He comes for a purpose, and we see clear examples of this in the Old Testament.

He filled people for artistic work. The Spirit of God filled Bezalel "with skill, ability and knowledge in all kinds of crafts—to make artistic designs for work in gold, silver and bronze, to cut and set stones, to work in wood, and to engage in all kinds of craftsmanship" (Exodus 31:3-5).

It is possible to be a talented musician, writer, or artist without being filled with the Spirit. But when the Spirit of God fills people for these tasks their work often takes on a new dimension. It has a different effect on others. It has a far greater spiritual impact. This can be true even where the natural ability of the musician or artist is not particularly outstanding. Hearts can be touched and lives changed. No doubt something like this happened through Bezalel.

He also filled individuals for the task of leadership. During the time of the Judges, the people of Israel were often overrun by various foreign nations. At one time it was the Midianites. God called Gideon to lead Israel. Gideon was very conscious of his own weakness and asked, "How can I save Israel? My clan is the weakest in Manasseh, and I am the least in my family" (Judges 6:15). Yet when the Spirit of God came upon Gideon (v. 34), he became one of the remarkable leaders of the Old Testament.

In leadership, God often uses those who feel weak, inadequate, and ill-equipped. When they are filled with the Spirit, they become outstanding leaders in the church.

In January 1955, Dr. Martin Luther King, Jr. was arrested for the first time. He was charged with driving at 30 mph in a 25 mph zone in his hometown of Montgomery, Alabama. This petty arrest was the climax of a season of sustained harassment by a racist police force. Authorities in Montgomery wanted to do everything possible to quench the fire lit by the Montgomery bus boycott, the first event of the civil rights movement. The boycott, aimed at ending segregation on the city's buses, had been organized by the Montgomery Improvement Association (MIA), of which King (a prominent clergyman in Montgomery) was president. After his arrest, King was released the same night. He returned home exhausted, but the phone rang immediately. It was yet another death threat, "Listen, nigger, we've taken all we want from you: before next week, you'll be sorry you ever came to Montgomery."

Unable to sleep, King made some coffee and sat down at the kitchen table. "I was ready to give up," he said. He was on the verge of quitting his presidency of the MIA, recalling later, "I felt myself growing in fear." But as he sat there, his face buried in his hands, he felt compelled to pray. "Something said to me, 'You've got to call on that something your daddy used to tell you about, that power that can make a way out of no way.'" King prayed, "Lord, I'm down here trying to do what's right. But I must confess that I'm weak now, I'm faltering. I'm losing my courage." At that moment King heard God's voice urging him to fight on. "He promised never to leave me." King was already a clergyman and preacher and doctoral student in theology. But it was only there in that kitchen in 1955 that "[he] experienced the presence of the Divine as [he] had never experienced Him before." From then on King said, "My uncertainty disappeared," and, "I was ready to face anything."

It was the Holy Spirit whom King experienced that night in the kitchen: "the power that can make a way out of no way." [54]

Elsewhere, we see the Holy Spirit filling people with strength and power. The story of Samson is well known. On one occasion, the Philistines tied him up by binding him with ropes. Then, "The Holy Spirit of the Lord came upon him in power. The ropes on his arms became like charred flax, and the bindings dropped from his hands" (Judges 15:14).

What is true in the Old Testament physically is often true in the New Testament and in our lives today, spiritually. It is not that we are physically bound by ropes, but that we are tied down by fears, habits, or addictions which take a grip on our lives. We are controlled by bad tempers or by patterns of thought such as envy, jealousy, or lust. We know that we are bound when we cannot stop something, even when we want to. When the Spirit of God came upon Samson, the ropes became like charred flax and he was free. The Spirit of God is able to set people free today from anything that binds them.

We experience the Holy Spirit not just so that we have a warm feeling in our hearts, but so that we go out and make a difference to our world. Later on we see how the Spirit of God came upon the prophet Isaiah to enable him "to preach good news to the poor . . . to bind up the brokenhearted, to proclaim freedom for the captives and release for the prisoners" and "to comfort all who mourn" (Isaiah 61:1-3).

We sometimes feel a sense of helplessness when confronted with the problems of the world. I often felt this before I was a Christian. I knew I had little or nothing to offer those whose lives were in a mess. I still feel like that sometimes. But I know that with the help of the Spirit of God, we do indeed have something to give. The Spirit of God enables us to bring the good news of Jesus Christ to bind up those with broken hearts; to proclaim freedom to those who are in captivity to things in their lives which deep down they hate; to release those who are imprisoned by their own wrongdoing; and to bring the comfort of the Holy Spirit (who is, after all, the Comforter) to those who are sad, grieving, or mourning. If we are going to help people in a way which lasts eternally, we cannot do so without the Spirit of God.

Promised by the Father

We have seen examples of the work of the Spirit of God in the Old Testament. But His activity was limited to particular people, at particular times, for particular tasks. As we go through the Old Testament we find that God promises He is going to do something new. The New Testament calls this "the promise of the Father." There is an increasing sense of anticipation. *What was going to happen?*

In the Old Testament, God made a covenant with His people. He said that He would be their God and that they would be His people. He required that they should keep His laws. They realized that they were good laws. Sadly, the people found that they were unable to keep His commands. The Old Covenant was consistently broken.

God promised that one day He would make a new covenant with His people. This covenant would be different from the first covenant: "I will put my law in their minds and write it on their hearts" (Jeremiah 31:33). In other words, under the New Covenant the law would be internal rather than external. If you go on a long hike, you start off by carrying your provisions on your back. They weigh you down and slow you up. But when you have eaten them, not only is the weight gone but you also have a new energy coming from inside. What God promised through Jeremiah was a time when the law would no longer be a weight on the outside but would become a source of energy from inside. *But how was all this going to happen?*

Ezekiel gives us the answer. He was a prophet, and God spoke through him, elaborating on the earlier promise: "I will give you a new heart and put a new spirit in you," he said. "I will remove from you your heart of stone and give you a heart of flesh. And I will put my Spirit in you and move you to follow my decrees and be careful to keep my laws" (Ezekiel 36:26-27).

Through the prophet Ezekiel, God was saying that this is what will happen when He puts His Spirit within us. This is how He will change our hearts and make them soft ("hearts of flesh") rather than hard ("hearts of stone"). The Spirit of God will move us to follow His decrees and keep His laws.

Jackie Pullinger has spent over thirty years working in what was the lawless walled city of Kowloon, Hong Kong. She has given her life to working with prostitutes, heroin addicts, and gang members. She began a memorable talk by saying, "God wants us to have soft hearts and hard feet. The trouble with many of us is that we have hard hearts and soft feet." Christians should have hard feet in that we should be tough rather than morally weak or "wet." Jackie is a glowing example of this in her willingness to go without sleep, food, and comfort in order to serve others. Yet she also has a soft heart: a heart filled with compassion. The toughness is in her feet, not her heart.

We have seen what "the promise of the Father" involves and how it is going to happen. Next, Joel tells us *to whom it is going to happen*. Through Joel, God says:

> I will pour out my Spirit on all people.
> Your sons and daughters will prophesy,
> your old men will dream dreams,
> your young men will see visions.
> Even on my servants, both men and women,
> I will pour out my Spirit in those days. (Joel 2:28-29)

Joel is foretelling that the promise will no longer be reserved for particular people, at particular times, for particular tasks, but it will be for all. God will pour out His Spirit regardless of sex ("sons and daughters . . . men and women"); regardless of age ("old men . . . young men"); regardless of background, race, color, or rank ("even on my servants"). There will be a new ability to hear God ("prophesy . . . dream . . . see visions"). Joel prophesied that the Spirit would be poured out with great generosity on all God's people.

Yet all these promises remained unfulfilled for at least 300 years. The people waited and waited for the "promise of the Father" to be fulfilled until at the coming of Jesus there was a burst of activity of the Spirit of God.

With the birth of Jesus, the trumpet sounds. Almost everyone connected with the birth of Jesus was filled with the Spirit of God. John the Baptist, who was to prepare the way, was filled with the Spirit even before his birth (Luke 1:15). Mary, Jesus' mother, was promised: "The Holy Spirit will come upon you, and the power of the Most High will overshadow you" (Luke 1:35). When Elizabeth, her cousin, came into the presence of Jesus, who was still in his mother's womb, she too was "filled with the Holy Spirit" (v. 41) and even John the Baptist's father Zechariah was "filled with the Holy Spirit" (v. 67). In almost every case there is an outburst of praise or prophecy.

John the Baptist links Him with Jesus

When John was asked whether he was the Christ he replied: "I baptize you with water. But one more powerful than I will come, the thongs of whose sandals I am not worthy to untie. He will baptize you with the Holy Spirit and with fire" (Luke 3:16). Baptism with water is very important, but it is not enough. Jesus is the Spirit baptizer. The Greek word means "to overwhelm," "to immerse," or "to plunge." It was the word used to describe a sinking ship when it had finally submerged. This is what should happen when we are filled with the Spirit. We should be completely overwhelmed by, immersed in, and plunged into the Spirit of God.

Sometimes this experience is like a hard, dry sponge being dropped into water. There can be a hardness in our lives which stops us absorbing the Spirit of God. It may take a little time for the initial hardness to wear off and for the sponge to be filled. So it is one thing for the sponge to be in the water ("baptized"), but it is another for the water to be in the sponge ("filled"). When the sponge is filled with water, the water literally pours out of it.

Jesus was a man completely filled with the Spirit of God. The Spirit of God descended on Him in bodily form at His baptism (Luke 3:22). He returned to the Jordan "full of the Holy Spirit" and was "led by the Spirit in the desert" (Luke 4:1). He returned to Galilee "in the power of the Spirit" (v. 14). In a synagogue in Nazareth he read the lesson from Isaiah 61:1, "The Spirit of the Lord is on me . . ." and said, "Today this scripture is fulfilled in your hearing" (v. 21).

Jesus predicted His presence

On one occasion Jesus went to a Jewish festival called the Feast of Tabernacles. Thousands of Jews would go to Jerusalem to celebrate the feast, looking back to the time when Moses brought water from a rock. They thanked God for providing water in the past year and prayed that He would do the same in the coming year. They looked forward to a time when water would pour out of the temple (as prophesied by Ezekiel), becoming deeper and deeper, and bringing life, fruitfulness, and healing wherever it went (Ezekiel 47).

This passage was read at the Feast of Tabernacles and enacted visually. The High Priest would go down to the pool of Siloam and fill a golden pitcher with water. He would then lead the people to the temple where he would pour water through a funnel in the west side of the altar, and into the ground, in anticipation of the great river that would flow from the temple. According to Rabbinic tradition, Jerusalem was the navel of the earth and the temple of Mount Zion was the center of the navel (its "belly" or "innermost being").

On the last day of the feast Jesus stood up and proclaimed, "If anyone thirsts, let him come to me and drink. He who believes in me, as the scripture has said, 'Out of his heart [the original word means 'belly' or 'innermost being'] shall flow rivers of living water'" (John 7:38, RSV). He was saying that the promises of Ezekiel and others would not be fulfilled in a place, but in a person. It is out of the innermost being of Jesus that the river of life will flow. So too, in a derivative sense, the streams of living water will flow from every Christian ("Whoever believes in me," v. 38). From us, Jesus says, this river will flow, bringing life, fruitfulness, and healing to others promised by God through Ezekiel.

John went on to explain that Jesus was speaking about the Holy Spirit "whom those who believed in him were later to receive" (v. 39). He added that "up to that time the Spirit had not been given" (v. 39). The promise of the Father had still not been fulfilled. Even after the crucifixion and resurrection of Jesus, the Spirit was not poured out. Later, Jesus told His disciples, "I am going to send you what my Father has promised; but stay in the city until you have been clothed with power from on high" (Luke 24:49).

Just before He ascended to heaven Jesus again promised, "You will receive power when the Holy Spirit comes on you" (Acts 1:8). But still they had to wait and pray for another ten days. Then at last, on the Day of Pentecost: "Suddenly a sound like the blowing of a violent wind came from heaven and filled the whole house where they were sitting. They saw what seemed to be tongues of fire that separated and came to rest on each of them. All of them were filled with the Holy Spirit and began to speak in other tongues as the Spirit enabled them" (Acts 2:2-4).

It had happened. The promise of the Father had been fulfilled. The crowd was amazed and mystified.

Peter stood up and explained what had occurred. He looked

back to the promises of God in the Old Testament and explained how all their hopes and aspirations were now being fulfilled before their eyes. He explained that Jesus had "received from the Father the promised Holy Spirit" and had "poured out what you now see and hear" (Acts 2:33).

When the crowd asked what they needed to do, Peter told them to repent and be baptized in the name of Jesus so that they could receive forgiveness. Then he promised that they would receive the gift of the Holy Spirit. For, he said, "The promise is for you and your children and for *all* who are far off—for all whom the Lord our God will call" (v. 39, italics mine).

We now live after Pentecost—the Spirit has been poured out. The promise of the Father has been fulfilled. Every single Christian receives the promise of the Father. It is no longer just for particular people, at particular times, for particular tasks. It is for *all* Christians, including you and me.

CHAPTER 9

WHAT DOES THE HOLY SPIRIT DO?

> Jesus answered, "I tell you the truth, no one can enter the kingdom of God unless he is born of water and the Spirit. Flesh gives birth to flesh, but the Spirit gives birth to spirit. You should not be surprised at my saying, 'You must be born again.' The wind blows wherever it pleases. You hear its sound, but you cannot tell where it comes from or where it is going. So it is with everyone born of the Spirit." (John 3:5-8)

A few years ago I was in a church in Brighton. One of the Sunday school teachers was telling us about her Sunday school class the previous week. She had been telling the children about Jesus' teaching on being born again in John 3:5-8. She was trying to explain to the children about the difference between physical birth and spiritual birth. In trying to draw them out on the subject she asked, "Are you born a Christian?" One little boy replied, "No, Miss. You are born normal!"

The expression "born again" has become something of a cliché. It was popularized in the United States and has even been used to advertise cars. Actually, Jesus was the first person to use the expression of people who were "born of the Spirit" (John 3:8).

A new baby is born as a result of a man and a woman joining together in sexual intercourse. In the spiritual realm, when the Spirit of God and the spirit of a man or woman come together, a new spiritual being is created. There is a new birth, spiritually. This is what Jesus is speaking about when He says, "You must be born again."

Jesus was saying that physical birth is not enough. We need to be born again by the Spirit. This is what happens when we become Christians. Every single Christian is born again. We may not be able to put our finger on the exact moment it occurred, but just as we know whether or not we are alive physically, so we should know that we are alive spiritually.

When we are born physically, we are born into a family. When we are born again spiritually, we are born into a Christian family. Much of the work of the Spirit can be seen in terms of a family. He assures us of our relationship with our Father and helps us to develop that relationship. He produces in us a family likeness. He unites us with our brothers and sisters, giving each member of the family different gifts and abilities. And He enables the family to grow in size.

In this chapter we will look at each of these aspects of His work in us as Christians. Until we become Christians the Spirit's work is primarily to convict us of our sin and our need for Jesus Christ, to convince us of the truth and to enable us to put our faith in Him (John 16:7-15). But we have a different type of relationship with the Holy Spirit when He comes to live within us. When I first became a Christian, I thought, "This is it! I've arrived!" I had been struggling with various issues, and then I made a decision to follow Christ. A friend had to explain to me that this was only the beginning.

Sons and daughters of God

The moment we come to Christ we receive complete forgiveness. The barrier between us and God has been removed. Paul says, "There is now no condemnation for those who are in Christ Jesus" (Romans 8:1). Jesus took all our sins—past, present, and future. God takes all our sins and buries them in the depths of the sea (Micah 7:19), and as the Dutch author Corrie Ten Boom used to say, "He puts up a sign saying 'No fishing.'"[55]

Not only does He wipe the slate clean, but He also brings us into a relationship with God as sons and daughters. Not all men and women are children of God in this sense, although all of us were created by God. It is only to those who receive Jesus, to those who believe in His name, that He gives the "right to become children of God" (John 1:12). Sonship in the New Testament (which today would include sons and daughters) is not a natural status, but a spiritual one. We become sons and daughters of God not by being born, but by being born again by the Spirit.

The Book of Romans has been described as the Himalayas of the New Testament. If this is the case, then chapter 8 is Mount Everest, and verses 14-17 could well be described as its peak.

> Because those who are led by the Spirit of God are sons of God. For you did not receive a spirit that makes you a slave again to fear, but you received the Spirit of sonship. And by him we cry, "Abba, Father." The Spirit himself testifies with our spirit that we are God's children. Now if we are children, then we are heirs—heirs of God and co-heirs with Christ, if indeed we share in his sufferings in order that we may also share in his glory. (Romans 8:14-17)

First of all, there is no higher privilege than to be a child of God. Under Roman law—which is probably what is in Paul's mind here—you could have no higher status than being adopted into a Roman family. If an adult wanted an heir he could either choose one of his own sons, or he could adopt a son. God has only one son—Jesus Christ— but He has many adopted children. There is a fairy story in which a reigning monarch adopts waifs and strays and makes them princes. In Christ, myth has become fact. We have been adopted into God's family. There could be no higher honor.

Billy Bray was a miner from Cornwall, born in 1794. He was an alcoholic and was always getting involved in fights and arguments at home. At the age of twenty-nine he became a Christian. He went home and told his wife, "You will never see me drunk again, by the help of the Lord." She never did. His words, his tone of voice, and his looks had magnetic power. He was charged with divine electricity. Crowds of miners would come and hear him preach. Many were converted and there were some remarkable healings. He was always praising God and saying that he had abundant reason to rejoice. He described himself as "a young prince." He was the adopted son of God, the King of kings, and therefore he was a prince, already possessing royal rights and privileges. His favorite expression was, "I am the son of a King."[56]

I met a Hungarian woman named Ildiko Papp. Eighteen months previously she had been a homeless alcoholic, living on the streets in a town near Budapest, when somebody invited her on an Alpha course. On that course she gave her life to Christ, experienced the love of Jesus, and was set free from alcoholism. When I asked her what difference Jesus had made to her life, she answered, "He's changed me from being a beggar to a princess."

Once we fully understand our status as adopted sons and daughters of God, we realize that there is no status in the world that even compares with the privilege of being a child of the Creator of the universe.

Secondly, as children we have the closest possible intimacy with God. Paul says that by the Spirit we cry, "*Abba*, Father!" This Aramaic word, *Abba* (that we looked at in the chapter "Why and How Do I Pray?"), is not found in the Old Testament. The use of this word in addressing God was distinctive of Jesus. It is impossible to translate it, but the nearest equivalent translation is probably "dear Father" or "Dad." The word speaks of the authority of the Father, as well as His accessibility. Jesus allows us to share in that intimate relationship with God when we receive His Spirit. "For you did not receive a spirit that makes you a slave again to fear, but you received the Spirit of sonship"

(v. 15). As Pope John Paul II said in an address to more than half a million young people in Poland just after the fall of Communism: "How can we fail to be amazed at the heights to which we are called? The human being, a created and limited being—even a sinner, is destined to be a child of God!"[57]

Prince Charles has many titles. He is the Heir Apparent to the Crown, his Royal Highness, the Prince of Wales, Duke of Cornwall, Knight of the Garter, Colonel in Chief of the Royal Regiment of Wales, Duke of Rothesay, Knight of the Thistle, Rear Admiral, Great Master of the Order of Bath, Earl of Chester, Earl of Carrick, Baron of Renfrew, Lord of the Isles, and Great Steward of Scotland. We would address him as "Your Royal Highness," but I suspect that to William and Harry he is simply "Dad." When we become children of God we have an intimacy with our heavenly King. John Wesley, the founder of Methodism, said about his conversion, "I exchanged the faith of a servant for the faith of a son."

Third, the Spirit gives us the deepest possible experience of God. "The Spirit himself testifies with our spirit that we are God's children" (v. 16). He wants us to know, deep within, that we are children of God. In the same way that I want my children to know and experience my love for them and my relationship with them, so God wants His children to be assured of that love and of that relationship.

One man who only experienced this quite late in his life is the South African Bishop Bill Burnett, who was at one time Archbishop of Capetown. I heard him say, "When I became a bishop I believed in theology [the truth about God], but not in God. I was a practical atheist. I sought righteousness by doing good." One day, after he had been a bishop for fifteen years, he went to speak at a confirmation service on the text in Romans, "God has poured out his love [i.e., his love for us] into our hearts by the Holy Spirit, whom he has given us" (Romans 5:5). After he had preached, he came home, poured himself a strong drink and was reading the paper when he felt the Lord saying, "Go and pray." He went into his chapel, knelt down in silence and sensed the Lord saying to him, "I want your body." He could not quite understand why (he is tall and thin and says, "I'm not exactly Mr. Universe"). However, he gave every part of himself to the Lord. "Then," He said, "what I preached about happened. I experienced electric shocks of love." He found himself flat on the floor and heard the Lord saying, "You are my son." When he got up, he knew indeed that something had happened. It proved a turning point in his life and ministry. Since then, through his ministry, many others have come to experience sonship through the witness of the Spirit.

Fourth, Paul tells us that to be a son or daughter of God is the greatest security. For if we are children of God we are also "heirs of God and co-heirs with Christ" (Romans 8:17). Under Roman law an adopted son would take his father's name and inherit his estate. As children of God we are heirs. The only difference is that we receive our final inheritance not on the death of our father, but on our own death. This is why Billy Bray was thrilled to think that "his heavenly Father had reserved everlasting glory and blessedness" for him. We will enjoy an eternity of love with Jesus.

Paul adds, "If indeed we share in his sufferings in order that we may also share in his glory" (v. 17). This is not a condition but an observation. Christians identify with Jesus Christ. This may mean some rejection and opposition here and now, but that is nothing compared to our inheritance as children of God.

Developing the relationship

Birth is not just the climax of a period of gestation, it is the beginning of a new life and new relationships. Our relationship with our parents grows and deepens over a long period. This happens as we spend time with them; it does not happen overnight.

Our relationship with God, as we have seen in the early chapters, grows and deepens as we spend time with Him. The Spirit of God helps us to develop our relationship with God. He brings us into the presence of the Father. "For through him [Jesus] we both [Jews and Gentiles alike] have access to the Father by one Spirit" (Ephesians 2:18). This is what it means for a Christian to experience God as Trinity. Through Jesus, by the Spirit, we have access to the presence of God. Jesus, through His death on the cross, removed the barrier between us and God. That is why we are able to come into God's presence. Often, we don't appreciate this when we are praying. We might feel there is a barrier but in fact there is none at all.

When I was at university I had a room above Barclays Bank on

High Street. We often used to have friends over for lunch in this room, and one day we were discussing whether or not the noise we made could be heard in the bank below. In order to find out, we decided to conduct an experiment. A girl named Kay went down into the bank. As it was lunchtime, it was packed with customers. The arrangement was that we would gradually build up the noise. First, one person would jump on the floor, then two, three, four, and eventually five. Next we would jump off chairs and then off the table. We wanted to see at which point we could be heard downstairs in the bank.

It turned out that the ceiling was thinner than we had thought. The first jump could definitely be heard. The second made a loud noise. After about the fifth, which sounded like a thunderstorm, there was total silence in the bank. Everyone had stopped cashing checks and was looking at the ceiling, wondering what was going on. Kay was right in the middle of the bank and thought, "What do I do? If I go out it's going to look very odd, but if I stay it is going to get worse!" She stayed. The noise built up and up. Eventually, bits of polystyrene started to fall from the ceiling. At that moment, fearing the ceiling would cave in, she rushed up to tell us that we could indeed be heard in the bank!

Imagine my surprise when I received a letter many years later from a man who had heard me tell this story on video. He said that he was interested in my reference to S1 and S2 Hewell's Court because he was the College Clerk of Works at the time: "The problem of sound penetration between S1 and S2 and Barclays Bank was reported to me, but until now I did not know who it was who had caused it. It was not polystyrene tiles that fell from the bank, but part of the suspended ceiling. Have no fear—there will not be any recrimination."

The barrier was much smaller than we thought! Since, through Jesus, the barrier has been removed, God hears us when we pray. We have immediate access to His presence, by the Spirit. We don't need to jump up and down to get His attention.

Not only does the Spirit bring us into the presence of God, He also helps us to pray. St. Paul writes, "the Spirit helps us in our weakness" (Romans 8:26). Sometimes we just don't know how to pray. But the Spirit Himself intercedes for us. What matters is not the place in which we pray, the position in which we pray, or whether or not we use set forms of prayer; what matters is whether or not we are praying in the Spirit. All prayer should be led by the Spirit. Without His help prayer can easily become lifeless and dull.

Another aspect of developing our relationship with God is understanding what He's saying to us. Again, the Spirit of God enables us to do this. Paul says, "I keep asking that the God of our Lord Jesus Christ, the glorious Father, may give you the Spirit of wisdom and revelation, so that you may know him better. I pray also that the eyes of your heart may be enlightened . . ." (Ephesians 1:17-18). The Spirit of God is a Spirit of wisdom and revelation. He opens our eyes so that, for example, we can understand what God is saying through the Bible.

Before I became a Christian I read and heard the Bible endlessly, in school services, at weddings and at funerals, but I did not understand it. It meant nothing to me. The reason it did not make sense to me was that I did not have the Spirit of God to interpret it. The Spirit of God is the best interpreter of what God has said.

Ultimately we will never understand Christianity without the Holy Spirit enlightening our eyes. We can see enough to make a step of faith, which is not a blind leap of faith, but real understanding often only follows faith. Anselm of Canterbury said, "I believe in order that I might understand."[58] Only when we believe and receive the Holy Spirit can we really understand God's revelation.

The Spirit of God helps us to develop our relationship with God and He enables us to sustain that relationship. People are often worried that they will not be able to keep going in the Christian life. God never intended for us to keep going by ourselves. By His Spirit, God keeps us going. It is the Spirit who brings us into a relationship with God and it is the Spirit who maintains that relationship. We are utterly dependent on Him.

The family likeness

I always find it fascinating to observe how children can look like both parents at the same time when the parents themselves may look so different. Even husbands and wives sometimes grow to look like each other as they spend time together over the years!

As we spend time in the presence of God, the Spirit of God

transforms us. As Paul writes, "And we, who with unveiled faces all reflect the Lord's glory, are being transformed into his likeness with ever-increasing glory, which comes from the Lord, who is the Spirit" (2 Corinthians 3:18). We are transformed into the moral likeness of Jesus Christ. The fruit of the Spirit is developed in our lives. Paul tells us that "the fruit of the Spirit is love, joy, peace, patience, kindness, goodness, faithfulness, gentleness and self-control" (Galatians 5:22). These are the characteristics that the Spirit of God develops in our lives. It is not that we become perfect immediately, but over a period of time there should be a change.

The first and most important fruit of the Spirit is love. Love lies at the heart of the Christian faith. The Bible is the story of God's love for us. His desire is that we should respond by loving Him and loving our neighbor. The evidence of the work of the Spirit in our lives will be an increasing love for God and an increasing love for others. Without this love everything else counts for nothing.

Second in Paul's list is joy. The journalist, Malcolm Muggeridge, wrote: "The most characteristic and uplifting of the manifestations of conversion is rapture—an inexpressible joy which suffuses our whole being, making our fears dissolve into nothing, and our expectations all move heavenwards."[59] This joy is not always mirrored by our outward circumstances. It comes from the Spirit within. Richard Wurmbrand, who was imprisoned for many years and frequently tortured on account of his faith, wrote of this joy: "Alone in my cell, cold, hungry and in rags, I danced for joy every night . . . sometimes I was so filled with joy that I felt I would burst if I did not give it expression."[60]

The third fruit listed is peace. Detached from Christ, inner peace is a kind of spiritual marshmallow full of softness and sweetness but without much actual substance. The Hebrew equivalent of the Greek word used here is *shalom*, which means "wholeness," "soundness," "well-being," "rootedness in community" and "relatedness to God." There is a longing within every human heart for peace like that. Epictetus, the first-century pagan thinker, said, "While the Emperor may give peace from war on land and sea, he is unable to give peace from passion, grief and envy. He cannot give peace of heart, for which man yearns more than ever for outward peace . . ."[61]

It is wonderful to see those whose characters have been transformed into the likeness of Jesus Christ as these and the other fruit of the Spirit—patience, kindness, goodness, and so on—have grown in their lives. A woman in her eighties in our congregation said of a former vicar, "He gets more and more like our Lord." I cannot think of a higher compliment than that. It is the work of the Spirit of God to make us more and more like Jesus so that we carry the knowledge of Him wherever we go (2 Corinthians 2:14).

Unity in the family

When we come to Christ and become sons and daughters of God we become part of a huge family. God's desire, like that of every normal parent, is that there should be unity in His family. Jesus prayed for unity among His followers (John 17). Paul pleaded with the Ephesian Christians to "make every effort to keep *the unity of the Spirit* through the bond of peace" (Ephesians 4:3, italics mine). The Spirit wants us to be united and helps us to grow in unity. We are meant to be an example in a troubled and divided world.

The same Holy Spirit lives in every Christian wherever they are and whatever their denomination, background, color, or race. The same Spirit is in every child of God and His desire is that we should be united. Indeed, that is what makes the divisions in the church such a tragedy, because there is "*one* body and *one* Spirit . . . *one* hope . . . *one* Lord, *one* faith, *one* baptism; *one* God and Father of *all*, who is over *all* and through *all* and in *all*" (Ephesians 4:4-6, italics mine).

The same Spirit indwells Christians in Russia, China, Africa, the United States, the U.K. or wherever. Roman Catholic, Orthodox, Lutheran, Methodist, Baptist, Pentecostal, Anglican, or nondenominational. In one sense, important as it may be to us, what matters more than our denomination is whether or not we have the Spirit of God. The same Spirit indwells Christians in every denomination. If people have the Spirit of God living within them, they are Christians, and our brothers and sisters. As Raniero Cantalamessa has said, "What unites us is infinitely greater than what divides us." It is a tremendous privilege to be part of this huge family; one of the great joys of coming to Christ is to experience this unity. There is a closeness and depth of relationship in the Christian church which I have never found outside of it. We must make every effort to keep the unity of the Spirit at every level: in our small groups, congregations, local churches, and the worldwide church.

Gifts for all the children

Although there is often a family likeness and, hopefully, unity in the family, there is also great diversity. No two children are identical—not even "identical" twins are exactly alike. So it is in the body of Christ. Every Christian is different; each has a different contribution to make, each has a different gift. In the New Testament there are lists of some of the gifts of the Spirit. In 1 Corinthians Paul lists nine gifts:

> Now to each one the manifestation of the Spirit is given for the common good. To one there is given through the Spirit the message of wisdom, to another the message of knowledge by means of the same Spirit, to another faith by the same Spirit, to another gifts of healing by that one Spirit, to another miraculous powers, to another prophecy, to another the distinguishing between spirits, to another speaking in different kinds of tongues, and to still another the interpretation of tongues. All these are the work of one and the same Spirit, and he gives them to each one, just as he determines. (1 Corinthians 12:7-11)

Elsewhere he mentions other gifts: those given to apostles, teachers, helpers, administrators (1 Corinthians 12:28-30), evangelists and pastors (Ephesians 4), gifts of serving, encouraging, giving, leadership, showing mercy (Romans 12:7), hospitality and speaking (1 Peter 4). No doubt these lists were not intended to be exhaustive.

All good gifts are from God, even if some, such as miracles, more obviously demonstrate the unusual acts of God in His world. Spiritual gifts include natural talents which have been transformed by the Holy Spirit. As the German theologian Jürgen Moltmann points out, "In principle every human potentiality and capacity can become charismatic [i.e., a gift of the Spirit] through a person's call, if only they are used in Christ."[62]

These gifts are given to all Christians. The expression "to each one" runs like a thread through 1 Corinthians 12. Every Christian is part of the body of Christ. There are many different parts, but one body (v. 12). We are baptized by (or in) one Spirit (v. 13). We are all given the one Spirit to drink (v. 13). There are no first- and second-class Christians. All Christians receive the Spirit. All Christians have spiritual gifts.

There is an urgent need for the gifts to be exercised. One of the major problems in the church at large is that so few are using their gifts. As a result, a few people are left doing everything and are totally exhausted, while the rest are under-utilized. The church has been likened to a soccer match, in which thousands of people desperately in need of exercise watch twenty-two people desperately in need of a rest!

The church will only operate with maximum effectiveness when every person is using his or her gifts. The Spirit of God gives each of us gifts. God does not require us to have many gifts, but He does require us to use what we have and to desire more (1 Corinthians 12:31; 14:1).

The growing family

It is natural for families to grow. God said to Adam and Eve, "Be fruitful and multiply." It should be natural for the family of God to grow. Again, this is the work of the Spirit. Jesus said, "You will receive power when the Holy Spirit comes on you; and you will be my witnesses in Jerusalem, and in all Judea and Samaria, and to the ends of the earth" (Acts 1:8).

The Spirit of God gives us both a desire and the ability to tell others. The playwright Murray Watts tells the story of a young man who was convinced of the truth of Christianity, but was paralyzed with fear at the very thought of having to admit to being "a Christian." The idea of telling anyone about his new-found faith, with all the dangers of being dubbed a religious nutcase, appalled him.

For many weeks he tried to banish the thought of religion from his mind, but it was no use. It was as if he heard a whisper in his conscience, repeating over and over again, "Follow me." At last he could stand it no longer and he went to a very old man, who had been a Christian for the best part of a century. He told him of his nightmare, this terrible burden of "witnessing to the light," and how it stopped him from becoming a Christian. The man sighed and shook his head. "This is a matter between you and Christ," he said. "Why bring all these other people into it?" The young man nodded slowly.

"Go home," said the old man. "Go into your bedroom alone. Forget the world. Forget your family, and make it a secret between you and God."

The young man felt a weight fall from him as the old man spoke. "You mean, I don't have to tell anyone?"

"No," said the old man.

"No one at all?"

"Not if you don't want to."

"Are you *sure*?" asked the young man, beginning to tremble with anticipation. "Can this be right?"

"It is right for you," said the old man.

So the young man went home, knelt down in prayer, and was converted to Christ. Immediately, he ran down the stairs and into the kitchen, where his wife, father, and three friends were sitting. "Do you realize," he said, breathless with excitement, "that it's possible to be a Christian without telling anyone?"[63]

When we experience the Spirit of God we want to tell others. As we do, the family grows. The Christian family should never be static. It should be continually growing and drawing in new people, who themselves receive the power of the Holy Spirit and go out and tell others about Jesus.

I have stressed throughout this chapter that the Holy Spirit lives in every Christian. Paul says, "And if anyone does not have the Spirit of Christ, he does not belong to Christ" (Romans 8:9). Yet not every Christian is filled with the Spirit. Paul writes to the Christians at Ephesus and says, "Be filled with the Spirit" (Ephesians 5:18). In the next chapter we will look at how we can be filled with the Spirit.

We started the previous chapter with Genesis 1:1-2 (the first verses in the Bible) and I want to end this chapter by looking at Revelation 22:17 (one of the last verses in the Bible). The Spirit of God is active throughout the Bible from Genesis to Revelation.

"The Spirit and the bride say, 'Come!' And let him who hears say, 'Come!' Whoever is thirsty, let him come; and whoever wishes, let him take the free gift of the water of life" (Revelation 22:17).

God wants to fill every one of us with His Spirit. Some people are longing for this. Some are not so sure that they want it—in which case they do not really have a thirst. If you do not have a thirst for more of the Spirit's fullness, why not pray for such a thirst? God takes us as we are. When we thirst and ask, God will give us "the free gift of the water of life."

CHAPTER 10

HOW CAN I BE FILLED WITH THE HOLY SPIRIT?

The evangelist J. John once addressed a conference on the subject of preaching. One of the points he made was that preachers often exhort their hearers to do something, but they never tell them *how* to do it. They say, "Read your Bible." He wants to ask, "Yes, but how?" They say, "Pray more." He asks, "Yes, but how?" They say, "Tell people about Jesus." He asks, "Yes, but how?" In this chapter I want to look at the question of *how* we can be filled with the Spirit.[64]

We have an old gas boiler in our house. The pilot light is on all the time, but the boiler is not always giving out heat and power. Some people have only got the pilot light of the Holy Spirit in their lives, whereas when people are filled with the Holy Spirit, they begin to fire on all cylinders. When you look at them you can almost see and feel the difference.

The Book of Acts has been described as Volume I of the history of the church. In it, we see several examples of people experiencing the Holy Spirit. In an ideal world every Christian would be filled with the Holy Spirit from the moment of conversion. Sometimes it happens like that (both in the New Testament and now), but not always—even in the New Testament. We have already looked at the first occasion of the outpouring of the Holy Spirit at Pentecost in Acts 2. As we go on through the Book of Acts we will see other examples.

When Peter and John prayed for the Samaritan believers and the Holy Spirit came upon them, Simon the Magician was so impressed that he offered money in order to be able to do the same thing (Acts

8:14-18). Peter warned him that it was a terrible thing to try to buy God's gift with money. But the account shows that something very wonderful must have happened.

In the next chapter (Acts 9) we see one of the most remarkable conversions of all times. When Stephen the first Christian martyr was stoned, Saul approved his death (Acts 8:1) and afterwards began to destroy the church. Going from house to house, he dragged men and women off to prison (v. 3). At the beginning of chapter 9 we find him still "breathing out murderous threats against the Lord's disciples."

Within the space of a few days, Saul was preaching in synagogues that "Jesus is the Son of God" (v. 20). He caused total astonishment, with people asking, "Isn't he the man who caused havoc in Jerusalem among those who call on this name [of Jesus]?"

What had happened in those few days to change him so completely? First, he had encountered Jesus on the road to Damascus. Secondly, he had been filled with the Spirit (v. 17). That moment, "something like scales fell from Saul's eyes, and he could see again" (v. 18). It sometimes happens that people who were not Christians, or who were even strongly anti-Christian, have a complete turnaround in their lives when they come to Christ and are filled with the Spirit. They can become powerful advocates of the Christian faith.

At Ephesus, Paul came across a group who "believed," but who had not even heard of the Holy Spirit. He placed his hands on them, the Holy Spirit came on them and they spoke in tongues and prophesied (Acts 19:1-7). There are people today who are in a similar position. They may have "believed" for some time or even all their lives. They may have been baptized, confirmed, and gone to church from time to time or even regularly. Yet they may know little or nothing about the Holy Spirit.

Another incident occurs early in the Book of Acts and I want to look at it in a little more detail. It is the first occasion when Gentiles were filled with the Spirit. God did something extraordinary, which started with a vision given to a man named Cornelius. God also spoke to Peter through a vision and told him He wanted him to go and speak to the Gentiles at the house of this man Cornelius. Halfway through Peter's talk, something remarkable happened: "The Holy Spirit came on all who heard the message. The circumcised believers [i.e., the

Jews] who had come with Peter were astonished that the gift of the Holy Spirit had been poured out even on the Gentiles. For they heard them speaking in tongues and praising God" (Acts 10:44-46). In the rest of the chapter I want to examine three aspects of what happened.

They experienced the power of the Holy Spirit

Peter had to stop his talk because it was obvious that something was happening. The filling of the Spirit rarely happens imperceptibly, although the experience is different for everyone.

In the description of the Day of Pentecost (Acts 2), Luke uses the language of a heavy tropical rainstorm. It is a picture of the power of the Spirit flooding their beings. There were physical manifestations. They heard a gale (v. 2) which was not a real gale, but it resembled one. It was the mighty invisible power of the *ruach* of God, reflecting the same word as we have seen for wind, breath, and spirit in the Old Testament. Sometimes, when people are filled, they shake like a leaf in the wind. Others find themselves breathing deeply, almost as if they were physically breathing in the Spirit.

They also saw what seemed to be tongues of fire that separated and came to rest on each of them (v. 3); in the Bible, fire signifies something powerful that purifies. Of course, it also sets things alight. Physical heat sometimes accompanies the filling of the Spirit and people experience it in their hands or some other part of their bodies. One person described a feeling of "glowing all over." Another said she experienced "liquid heat." Still another described "burning in my arms when I was not hot." Fire perhaps symbolizes the power, passion, and purity that the Spirit of God brings to our lives.

For many, the experience of the Spirit may be an overwhelming experience of the love of God. Paul prays for the Christians at Ephesus that they might have "power, together with all the saints, to grasp how wide and long and high and deep is the love of Christ" (Ephesians 3:18). The love of Christ is wide enough to reach every person in the world. It reaches across every continent to people of every race, color, tribe, and background. It is long enough to last throughout a lifetime and into eternity. It is deep enough to reach us however far we have fallen. It is high enough to lift us into the heavenly places. We see this love supremely in the cross of Christ. We know Christ's love for us because He was willing to die for us. Paul prayed that we would "grasp" the extent of this love.

Yet he does not stop there. He goes on to pray that we would "*know* this love that *surpasses knowledge*"—that you would be filled to the measure of all the fullness of God" (Ephesians 3:19, italics mine). It is not enough to understand His love; we need to experience His love that "surpasses knowledge." It is often as people are filled with the Spirit—"filled to the measure of all the fullness of God" (v. 19) that they experience in their heart this transforming love of Christ.

Thomas Goodwin, one of the Puritans of 300 years ago, illustrated this experience. He pictured a man walking along a road, hand in hand with his son. The little boy knows that this man is his father, and that his father loves him. But suddenly the father stops, picks up the boy, lifts him into his arms, embraces him, kisses him and hugs him. Then he puts him down again, and they continue walking. It is a wonderful thing to be walking along holding your father's hand, but it is an incomparably greater thing to have his arms enfolded around you.

"He has embraced us," says Spurgeon and He pours His love upon us and He "hugs" us. Martyn Lloyd-Jones quotes these examples among many others in his book on Romans, and comments on the experience of the Spirit:

> Let us realize then the profound character of the experience. This is not light and superficial and ordinary; it is not something of which you can say, "Don't worry about your feelings." Worry about your feelings? You will have such a depth of feeling that for a moment you may well imagine that you have never "felt" anything in your life before. It is the profoundest experience that a man can ever know.[65]

They were released in praise

When these Gentiles were filled with the Spirit they started "praising God." Spontaneous praise is the language of people who are excited about their experience of God.

I am asked, "Is it right to express emotions in church? Isn't there a danger of emotionalism?" The danger for most of us in our relationship with God is not that there is too much emotion, but too little. Our relationship with God can be rather cold. Every relationship of love involves our emotions. Of course, there must be more than emotions. There must be friendship, communication, understanding, and service. But if I never showed any emotion towards my wife, there would be something lacking in my love for her. If we do not experience any emotion in our relationship with God, then our whole personality is not involved.

St. Augustine said this about God: "The thought of you stirs a person so deeply that they cannot be content unless they praise you, because you have made us for yourself, and our hearts are restless until they rest in you."[66] Worship is the purpose for which we were made. As the Westminster Catechism puts it, "A man's chief end is to glorify God and to enjoy him for ever." It should involve our whole personality, including our emotions. We are called to love, praise, and worship God with *all* of our beings.

"Well clearly there was no football in Saint Augustine's day."

It could be argued that emotions are all right in private, but what about the public demonstration of emotion? After a conference attended by George Carey when he was Archbishop of Canterbury there was a correspondence in *The Times* about the place of emotions in church. One man wrote:

> Why is it that if a cinema comedy produces laughter, the film is regarded as successful; if a theatre tragedy brings tears to the audience the production is regarded as touching; if a football match thrills the spectators, the game is reviewed as exciting; but if the congregation are moved by the glory of God in worship, the audience are accused of emotionalism?

Of course, there is such a thing as emotionalism, where emotions take precedence over the solid foundation of teaching from the Bible. But as the former Bishop of Coventry, Cuthbert Bardsley, once said, "The chief danger of the Anglican church is not delirious emotionalism." Our worship is the expression of our love for God and it should involve our whole beings: our mind, heart, will, and emotions.

They received a new language

As on the Day of Pentecost and with the Christians in Ephesus (Acts 19), when the Gentiles were filled with the Spirit they received the gift of tongues. The word for "tongues" is the same word as that for "languages" and it means the ability to speak in a language you have never learned. It may be an angelic language (1 Corinthians 13:1), which presumably is not recognizable, or it may be a recognizable human language (as at Pentecost). A young woman in our congregation, named Penny, was praying with another girl. She ran out of words in English and started praying in tongues. The girl smiled and then opened her eyes and started laughing. She said, "You have just spoken to me in Russian." The girl, although English, spoke fluent Russian and had a great love for the language. Penny asked, "What have I been saying?" The girl told her that she had been saying, "My dear child," over and over again. Penny does not speak a single word of Russian. For that young woman, those three words were of great significance. She was assured that she was important to God.

The gift of tongues has brought great blessing to many people. It is, as we have seen, one of the gifts of the Spirit. It is not the only gift or even the most important gift. Not all Christians speak in tongues, nor is it a necessary sign of being filled with the Spirit. It is possible to be filled with the Spirit and not speak in tongues. Nevertheless, for many, both in the New Testament and in the Christian life more generally, it accompanies an experience of the Holy Spirit and may be the first experience of the more obviously supernatural activity of the Spirit. Many today are puzzled by the gift. This is why I have devoted quite a lot of space in this chapter to the subject. In 1 Corinthians 14, Paul deals with a number of questions that are often raised.

What exactly is speaking in tongues?

It is a form of prayer (one of the many different forms of prayer found in the New Testament) according to Paul, "for anyone who speaks in a tongue does not speak to men but *to God*" (1 Corinthians 14:2, italics mine). It is a form of prayer that builds up the individual Christian (v. 4). The gifts which directly edify the church are obviously even more important, but this does not make tongues unimportant. The benefit of tongues is that it is a form of prayer which transcends the limitation of human language. This seems to be what Paul means when he says, "For if I pray in a tongue, my spirit prays, but my mind is unfruitful" (1 Corinthians 14:14).

Everybody, to a greater or lesser extent, is limited by language. I'm told that the average native English speaker has a vocabulary of between 10,000 and 20,000 words. Winston Churchill, however, had a vocabulary of around 50,000 words. But even he was limited to that extent. People often experience frustration that they cannot express what they really feel, even in a human relationship. They feel things in their spirits, but they do not know how to put them into words. This is also often true in our relationship with God.

This is where the gift of tongues can be a great help. It enables us to express to God what we really feel in our spirits without going through the process of translating it into English. (Hence Paul says, "my mind is unfruitful.") It is not mindless; the speaker is in full control, and can start and stop where they want. However, the mind is "unfruitful," because it is not going through the process of translation into an intelligible language.

In what areas does it help?

There are three areas in which many people have found this gift especially helpful.

First, in the area of *praise and worship*. We are particularly limited in our language. When children (or even adults) write thank-you letters, it is not long before they run out of language, and we find that words such as "lovely," "wonderful," or "brilliant" are repeated over and over again. In our praise and worship of God we can often find language limiting.

We long to express our love, worship, and praise of God, particularly when we are filled with the Spirit. The gift of tongues enables us to do this without the limitation of human language.

Second, it can be a great help when *praying under pressure*. There are times in our lives when it is hard to know exactly how to pray. It can be because we are burdened by pressure, anxiety, or grief. I prayed for a twenty-six-year-old widower whose wife had died of cancer a year into their marriage. He asked for, and instantly received, the gift of tongues while we were praying. All the grief, sadness, and emotion that he had pushed down in his life seemed to pour out as he prayed. He told me afterwards what a relief it had been to be able to unburden all those things.

I too have found this in my own experience. In 1987, during a staff meeting at our church, I received a message to say that my mother had had a heart attack and was in hospital. As I dashed up to the main road and caught a taxi to the hospital, I have never been more grateful for the gift of tongues. I desperately wanted to pray, but felt too shocked to form any sentences in English. The gift of tongues enabled me to pray all the way to the hospital and to bring the situation to God in a time of crisis.

Third, many people have found the gift a help in *praying for other people*. It is hard to pray for others—especially if you have not seen them or heard from them for some time. After a while, "Lord, bless them" might be our most elaborate prayer. It can be a real help to start praying in tongues for them. Often, as we do that, God gives us the words to pray in English.

It is not selfish to want to pray in tongues. Although "he who speaks in a tongue edifies himself" (1 Corinthians 14:4), the indirect effects of this can be very great. Jackie Pullinger describes the transformation in her ministry when she began to use the gift:

> By the clock I prayed 15 minutes a day in the language of the Spirit and still felt nothing as I asked the Spirit to help me intercede for those he wanted to reach. After about six weeks of this I began to lead people to Jesus without trying. Gangsters fell to their knees sobbing in the streets, women were healed, heroin addicts were miraculously set free. And I knew it all had nothing to do with me.

It was also the gateway for her to receive other gifts of the Spirit:

> With my friends I began to learn about the other gifts of the Spirit and we experienced a remarkable few years of ministry. Scores of gangsters and well-to-do people, students and churchmen, were converted and all received a new language to pray in private and other gifts to use when meeting together. We opened several homes to house heroin addicts and all were delivered from drugs painlessly because of the power of the Holy Spirit.[67]

Does Paul approve of speaking in tongues?

The context of 1 Corinthians 14 is excessive public use in church of the gift of tongues. Paul says, "*In the church* I would rather speak five intelligible words to instruct others than ten thousand words in a tongue" (v. 19, italics mine). There would be little point in Paul arriving at Corinth and giving his sermon in tongues. They would not be able to understand unless there was someone to interpret. So he lays down guidelines for the public use of tongues (v. 27).

Nevertheless, Paul makes it clear that speaking in tongues should not be forbidden (v. 39). With regard to the private use of this gift (on our own with God), he strongly encourages it. He says, "I would like every one of you to speak in tongues" (v. 5) and, "I thank God that I speak in tongues more than all of you" (v. 18). This does not mean that every Christian has to speak in tongues or that we are second-class Christians if we do not speak in tongues. There is no such thing as first- or second-class Christians. Nor does it mean that God loves us any less if we don't yet speak in tongues. Nevertheless, the gift of tongues is a blessing from God.

How do we receive the gift of tongues?

Some say, "I don't want the gift of tongues." God will never force you to receive a gift. Tongues is just one of the wonderful gifts of the Spirit, and not the only one by any means, as we saw in the last chapter. Like every gift, it has to be received by faith.

Not every Christian speaks in tongues, but there is no reason why anyone who wants this gift should not receive it. Paul is not saying that speaking in tongues is the be-all and end-all of the Christian life; he is saying that it is a very helpful gift. If you would like to receive it, there is no reason why you should not.

Like all the gifts of God, we have to co-operate with His Spirit. God does not force His gifts on us. When I first prayed for the gift, I kept my mouth firmly shut! Then someone explained to me that if I wanted to receive the gift of tongues, I had to co-operate with the Spirit of God, open my mouth and start to speak to God in a language other than English or any another known to me. As I did, the words began to come and I received the gift of tongues also.

What are the common hindrances to being filled with the Spirit?

On one occasion Jesus was speaking to His disciples on the subject of prayer and the Holy Spirit (Luke 11:9-13). In that passage He deals with some of the principal difficulties we may have in receiving from God.

Doubt

There are many doubts people have in this whole area, the principal one being, "If I ask, will I receive?" Jesus says simply: "I say to you: Ask and it will be given to you" (Luke 11). Jesus must have seen that they were a little skeptical because He repeats it in a different way: "Seek and you will find."

And again He says a third time: "Knock and the door will be opened to you."

He knows human nature so He goes on a fourth time: "For everyone who asks receives."

They are not convinced, so He says it a fifth time: "He who seeks finds."

Again a sixth time: "To him who knocks, the door will be opened."

Why does He say it six times? Because He knows what we are like. We find it very difficult to believe that God would give us anything—let alone something as unusual and wonderful as His Holy Spirit and the gifts that come with the Spirit.

Fear

Even if we have cleared the first hurdle of doubt, some of us trip up on the next hurdle of fear. The fear is about what we will receive. Will it be something good?

Jesus uses the analogy of a human father. If a child asks for a fish, no father would give him a snake. If a child asks for an egg, no father would give him a scorpion (Luke 11:11-12). It is unthinkable that we would treat our children like that. Jesus goes on to say that in comparison with God we are evil! If we would not treat our children like that, it is inconceivable that God would treat us like that. He is not going to let us down. If we ask for the Holy Spirit and all the wonderful gifts He brings, that is exactly what we will receive (Luke 11:13).

Inadequacy

Of course, it is important that there is no unforgiveness or other sin in our lives, and that we have turned our back on all that we know is wrong. However, even after we have done that, we often have a vague feeling of unworthiness and inadequacy. We cannot believe that God would give us anything. We can believe that He would give gifts to very "advanced" Christians, but not to us. But Jesus does not say, "How much more will your Father in heaven give the Holy Spirit to all very 'advanced' Christians." He says, "How much more will your Father in heaven give the Holy Spirit to *those who ask him*" (Luke 11:13, italics mine).

If you would like to be filled with the Spirit you might like to find someone who would pray for you. If you don't have anyone who would be able to pray for you, there is nothing to stop you from praying on your own. Some are filled with the Spirit without receiving the gift of tongues. The two do not necessarily go together. Yet in the New Testament and in experience they often do go together. There is no reason why we should not pray for both.

If you are praying on your own:

1. Ask God to forgive you for anything that could be a barrier to receiving.

2. Turn from any area of your life that you know is wrong.

3. Ask God to fill you with His Spirit. Go on seeking Him until you find. Go on knocking until the door opens. Seek God with all your heart.

4. If you would like to receive the gift of tongues, ask. Then open your mouth and start to praise God in any language but English or any other language known to you.

5. Believe that what you receive is from God. Don't let anyone tell you that you made it up. (It is most unlikely that you have.)

6. Persevere. Languages take time to develop. Most of us start with a very limited vocabulary. Gradually it develops. Tongues is like that. It takes time to develop the gift. But don't give up.

7. If you have prayed for any other gift, seek opportunities to use it. Remember that all gifts have to be developed by use.

Being filled with the Spirit is not a one-time experience. Peter was filled with the Spirit three times in the space of chapters 2–4 in the Book of Acts (Acts 2:4; 4:8, 31). When Paul says, "Be filled with the Spirit" (Ephesians 5:18), he uses the present continuous tense, urging them and us to go on and on being filled with the Spirit.

CHAPTER 11

HOW CAN I RESIST EVIL?

There is a close connection between good and God and between evil and the devil. Indeed, in each case the difference is only one letter! Behind the power of good lies Goodness Himself. Directly or indirectly behind our own evil desires and the temptations of the world lies evil personified—the devil.

Because there is so much evil in the world, some find it easier to believe in the devil than in God. "As far as God goes, I am a non-believer . . . but when it comes to the devil—well that's something else . . . the devil keeps advertising . . . the devil does lots of commercials," said William Peter Blatty who wrote and produced *The Exorcist*.[68]

On the other hand, many Westerners find belief in the devil more difficult than belief in God. This may be partly because of a false image of what the devil is like. If the image of God as a white-bearded old man sitting on a cloud is absurd and incredible, so also is the image of a horned devil with cloven hooves and a forked tail.

Once we have come to believe in a transcendent God, in some ways it is only logical to accept belief in a devil.

> Belief in a great transcendent power of evil adds nothing whatever to the difficulties imposed by belief in a transcendent power of good. Indeed, it eases them somewhat. For if there were no Satan, it would be hard to resist the conclusion that God is a fiend both because of what he does, in nature, and what he allows, in human wickedness.[69]

According to the biblical worldview, behind the evil in the world there lies the devil. The Greek word for the devil, *diabolos*, translates the Hebrew word *satan*. We are not told very much about the origins of Satan in the Bible. There is a hint that he may be a fallen angel (Isaiah 14:12-23). He appears on a few occasions in the books of the Old Testament (Job 1; 1 Chronicles 21:1). He is not merely a force but is personal.

We are given a clearer picture of his activities in the New Testament. There we see that the devil is a personal, spiritual being who is in active rebellion against God and has the leadership of many demons like himself. Paul tells us to take our "stand against the devil's schemes. For our struggle is not against flesh and blood, but against the rulers, against the authorities . . . against the spiritual forces of evil in the heavenly realms" (Ephesians 6:11-12).

The devil and his angels, according to Paul, are not to be underestimated. They are cunning ("the devil's schemes" v. 11). They are powerful ("rulers," "authorities," and "forces" v. 12). They are evil ("forces of evil" v. 12). We should, therefore, not be surprised when we come under a powerful assault from the enemy.

Why should we believe in the devil?

First, it is biblical. That is not to say that the Bible concentrates on the devil. Satan is not mentioned very often in the Old Testament and it is only when we come to the New Testament that the doctrine is developed more fully. Jesus clearly believed in the existence of Satan and was tempted by him. He frequently cast out demons, freeing people from the forces of evil and sin in their lives, and gave His disciples authority to do the same. In the Lord's Prayer, He taught us to pray, "Deliver us from the evil one." In the rest of the New Testament there are many references to the work of the devil (1 Peter 5:8-11; Ephesians 6:1-12).

Second, Christians down the ages have almost invariably believed in the existence of the devil. The early church theologians, the Reformers, the great evangelists like Wesley and Whitefield, and the overwhelming majority of men and women of God, knew that there were very real spiritual forces of evil around. As soon as we start to serve the Lord, the devil's interest is aroused. New believers can be surprised to find that they experience increased temptation having put their faith in Christ.

Third, it makes sense of the world; it is reasonable to believe in the existence of the devil. Any kind of worldview that ignores the existence of a personal devil has a great deal to explain: evil regimes, institutional torture and violence, mass murders, brutal rapes, large scale drug-trafficking, terrorist atrocities, sexual and physical abuse of children, occult activity and satanic rituals.

On March 13, 1996, forty-four-year-old Thomas Hamilton entered the elementary school gym in Dunblane, Scotland, and opened fire on a class of five- and six-year-olds. This is only one of many such terrible school massacres that have taken place around the world in recent years. On this occasion, a teacher and sixteen children were killed, and seventeen wounded. The principal said this: "Evil has visited our school."

Scripture, tradition, and reason then, all point to the existence of the devil. However, this does not mean that we need to become obsessed by the subject. As C. S. Lewis points out, "There are two equal and opposite errors into which our race can fall about the devils. One is to disbelieve in their existence. The other is to believe, and to feel an excessive and unhealthy interest in them. They themselves are equally pleased by both errors and hail a materialist or a magician with the same delight."[70]

In our society today there is a significant interest in the demonic, be it spiritualism, fortune-telling, ouija boards, consulting the dead, astrology, horoscopes, witchcraft, or occult powers. Involvement in these things is expressly forbidden in Scripture (Deuteronomy 18:10; Leviticus 19:20ff; Galatians 5:19ff; Revelation 21:8; 22:15). Of course, many of us may have been involved in these activities in the past. Before I was a Christian, I didn't think there was any harm in playing around with ouija boards; it just seemed something fun. Many people also explore these things because they find themselves searching for a spiritual experience and don't know where to look. Thankfully, though, these are not unforgivable sins. If we have meddled in any of these things, we can be forgiven. We need to repent and get rid of anything associated with that activity such as books, charms, DVDs, or magazines (Acts 19:19).

Christians, too, can have an unhealthy interest in these things. A new Christian once showed me a couple of supposedly Christian books, in which the whole emphasis was on the work of the devil—with a lot of space devoted to speculation concerning the number of the beast in Revelation, and tying this in with credit cards! The intention was good, I am sure, but the focus on the work of the enemy seemed to me to be unhealthy. The Bible never has this kind of focus. The spotlight is always on God.

What are the devil's tactics?

The ultimate aim of Satan is to destroy every human being. Jesus said, "the thief comes only to steal and kill and destroy . . ." (John 10:10). The devil wants us to follow a path that leads to destruction. To that end, he tries to prevent anyone coming to faith in Jesus Christ. Paul tells us: "The god of this age [the devil] has blinded the minds of unbelievers, so that they cannot see the light of the gospel of the glory of Christ, who is the image of God" (2 Corinthians 4:4).

So long as we are going along Satan's path and our eyes are blinded, we will probably be almost totally unaware of his tactics. Once we start walking along the path that leads to life and our eyes are opened to the truth, we become aware that we are under attack. The initial line of attack is often in the area of doubt. We see this in the opening chapters of Genesis where the enemy, in the form of a serpent, says to Eve, "Did God *really* say . . . ?" His opening move is to raise a doubt in her mind.

We see the same tactic in the temptation of Jesus. The devil comes to him and says, "*If* you are the Son of God . . ." (Matthew 4:3, italics mine). First, he raises doubts, then come the temptations. His tactics have not changed. He still raises doubts in our mind: "Did God *really* say that such and such a course of action is wrong?" or, "*If* you are a Christian . . ." He tries to undermine our confidence in what God has said and in our relationship with Him. We need to recognize this source of many of our doubts.

Raising doubts was the precursor to the main attack on both Eve in the Garden of Eden and Jesus in the wilderness. Satan is sometimes described as "the tempter" (Matthew 4:2) and in Genesis 3, we see an exposé of how he works.

In Genesis 2:16-17, God gave Adam and Eve a far-reaching permission ("You are free to eat from any tree in the garden"), one prohibition ("But you must not eat from the tree of the knowledge of good and evil") and then warned them of the penalty if they disobeyed ("For when you eat of it you will surely die").

Satan ignores the wide scope of the permission and concentrates on the one prohibition, which he then exaggerates (Genesis 3:1). His tactics have not changed. He still ignores the permission. He ignores the fact that God has given us all things richly to enjoy (1 Timothy 6:17). He ignores the amazing privilege of a relationship with God: the transformation of relationships, the enriching of our lives and countless other things that God offers to those who know and love Him. He also ignores all the wonderful things that God gives everybody: relationships, families, the whole of creation, the stunning beauty of our world, art, music, literature, sport, food and drink; all the guiltless pleasures. He does not tell us about these things. Instead he concentrates on a tiny unimaginative list of prohibitions of what Christians are not allowed to do, reminding us again and again that we can't take drugs, cheat on our expenses, or be promiscuous. There are relatively few things that God does not allow us to do and there are very good reasons why He prohibits them.

Finally, Satan denies the penalty. He says, "You will not surely die" (Genesis 3:4). He says, in effect, that it will not do you any harm to disobey God. He suggests to us that God is really a spoilsport, that God does not want the best for our lives and that we will miss out if we don't disobey. In fact, the opposite is the case, as Adam and Eve found out. It is disobedience which causes us to miss out on so much of what God intended for us.

In the verses that follow, we see the consequences of disobeying God. First, there is shame and embarrassment. Adam and Eve felt exposed and began a cover-up operation (v. 7). How quickly would we want to leave the room if every action we had ever done was displayed on a screen, followed by a written list of every thought we had ever entertained? Deep down, we all feel ashamed and embarrassed by our sin. We don't want people to find us out. Sir Arthur Conan Doyle, creator of the *Sherlock Holmes* stories, once played a practical joke on twelve men. They were all very well-known, respected, and respectable men, regarded as pillars of the establishment. He sent each of them a telegram, with the same message in each: "Flee at once.

All is discovered." Within twenty-four hours, they had all fled the country! Virtually all of us have something in our lives of which we are ashamed; something we would not want everyone to know about. We often put up barriers around us to avoid the possibility of being found out.

Next, Adam and Eve's friendship with God was broken. When they heard God coming, they hid (v. 8). Many people today shy away from God. They don't want to face up to the possibility of His existence. Like Adam, they are afraid (v. 10). Some have a real fear of going to church or mingling with Christians. A couple in our congregation told me about a sixteen-stone rugby player from Australia whom they had invited to church. He got as far as the driveway, then he started shaking in the car. He said, "I can't go. I'm too frightened to go into the church." He could not look God in the face. There was a separation between him and God, just as there was with Adam and Eve. God immediately started to try to draw them back into a relationship. He called out, "Where are you?" (v. 9). He still does.

Then, there is a separation between Adam and Eve themselves. Adam blames Eve. Eve blames the devil. But they, and we, are responsible for our own sin. We cannot blame God, or others, or even the devil (James 1:13-15). We see this in our society today. When people turn away from God, they start fighting one another. We see the breakdown of relationships wherever we look: broken marriages, broken homes, broken relationships at work, civil war, and global conflicts.

Finally, we see in the description of God's punishment of Adam and Eve (v. 14 onwards) that they had been deceived by Satan. We see how this deception led Adam and Eve away from God and onto a pathway that Satan knew, from the beginning, led to destruction.

We see that Satan is a tempter, one who raises doubts, a deceiver, and a destroyer. He is also an accuser. The Hebrew word for Satan means "accuser" or "slanderer." He accuses God before people. God gets the blame for everything. God, he says, is not to be trusted. Secondly, he accuses Christians before God (Revelation 12:10). He denies the power of the death of Jesus. He condemns us and makes us feel guilty—not for any particular sin, but with a general and vague feeling of guilt. In contrast, when the Holy Spirit draws attention to a sin, He identifies it so that we can turn from it.

Temptation is not the same thing as sin. Sometimes the devil puts a thought into our mind, which we know is wrong. At that moment we have a choice whether to accept it or reject it. If we accept it, we are on the way towards sin. If we reject it, we do what Jesus did. He was "tempted in every way, just as we are—yet was without sin" (Hebrews 4:15). When Satan put evil thoughts in His mind, He rejected them. But often before we have the chance to decide one way or the other, Satan accuses us. Within a split second he says, "Look at you! Call yourself a Christian? What was that you were thinking about? You can't be a Christian. What a terrible thing to think!" He wants us to agree and say, "Oh no! I can't be a Christian," or, "Oh no! I've blown it now, so it doesn't matter if I blow it a bit more!" We are on a downward slope, and this is his aim. The tactics are those of condemnation and accusation. If he can provoke guilt in us, he knows that we may think: "It doesn't really make any difference now if I do it or not. I have already failed." So we do it and temptation becomes sin.

He wants failure to become a pattern in our lives. He knows that the more we fall into sin, the more sin will start to control our lives. The first injection of heroin may not be enough to get a grip, but if you inject it day after day, month after month, year after year, it gets a grip and you become an addict. It has taken hold of you. If we fall into a pattern of doing things which we know to be wrong, these things grip our lives. We become addicted and we are on the path that Satan desires—the one that leads to destruction (Matthew 7:13).

What is our position?

As Christians, God has rescued us from "the dominion of darkness and brought us into the kingdom of the Son he loves" (Colossians 1:13). Before we were Christians, Paul says, we were in the dominion of darkness. Satan ruled us and we were subject to sin, slavery, death, and destruction. That is what the dominion of darkness is like.

Now, Paul says, we have been transferred to the kingdom of light. The moment we come to Christ we are transferred from darkness to light and, in the kingdom of light, Jesus is King. There is forgiveness, freedom, life, and salvation. Once we have been transferred, we belong to someone else: to Jesus Christ and His kingdom.

In 2003, the Spanish football club Real Madrid paid £24.5 million for David Beckham to be transferred from Manchester United to Real Madrid. Imagine that Beckham, while playing for Real Madrid, one day received a phone-call from Alex Ferguson, his previous manager at Manchester United, saying, "Why weren't you at the practice this morning?" He would have said, "I don't work for you any more. I have been transferred. I am working for another club."

In a far more wonderful way, we have been transferred from the kingdom of darkness where Satan is in charge, to the kingdom of God where Jesus is in charge. When Satan asks us to do his work our reply is, "I don't belong to you any more."

Satan is a conquered foe (Luke 10:17-20). On the cross, Jesus "disarmed the powers and authorities" and "made a public spectacle of them, triumphing over them by the cross" (Colossians 2:15). Satan and all his minions were defeated at the cross, and that is why Satan and his demons are so frightened of the name of Jesus (Acts 16:18). It reminds them of their defeat.

The cross was the great victory over Satan, and we now live in the time of the mopping-up operations. Although the enemy is not yet destroyed and is still capable of inflicting casualties, he is disarmed, defeated, and demoralized. The day will come when Jesus returns and Satan is finally destroyed.

The situation we are in is similar to the difference between D-Day and VE-Day at the end of the Second World War. D-Day, June 6, 1944, was the decisive battle and it determined the outcome of the war. After D-Day there was no real doubt about the coming victory—yet it was not over. The mopping up operations continued until VE-Day on May 8, 1945. In a sense, Christians live between D-Day (the cross) and VE-Day (Jesus' return). Satan is a conquered enemy, yet he is still around.

Jesus has freed us from guilt, so we don't need to be condemned. He has set us free from addictions. Jesus broke the power of these things and set us free. He broke the fear of death when He defeated death. With that, He set us free, potentially, from every fear. All these things—guilt, addiction, and fear—belong to the kingdom of darkness. Jesus has transferred us to a new kingdom.

When I became a Christian, I found there were some things that I was set free from almost immediately. However, there are other things that I still struggle with. My battle will not finally be won until Jesus returns.

This, then, is our position, and it is vital to realize the strength of the position we are in, due to the victory of Jesus on the cross for us.

How do we defend ourselves?

Since the war is not over and Satan is not yet destroyed, we need to make sure that our defenses are in order. Paul tells us to "put on the full armor of God so that you can take your stand against the devil's schemes" (Ephesians 6:11). He then mentions six pieces of equipment that we need. Sometimes it is said, "The secret of the Christian life is . . ." But there is no one secret; we need *all* the armor.

First, we need the "belt of truth" (v. 14). This probably means the foundation of Christian doctrine and truth. It means getting the whole Christian truth (or as much of it as one can) into one's system. We do this by reading the Bible, listening to sermons and talks, reading Christian books, and listening to CDs or downloads. This will enable us to distinguish what is true, and what are Satan's lies, for Satan is "a liar and the father of lies" (John 8:44).

Next, we need the breastplate of righteousness (v. 14). This is the righteousness that comes from God through what Jesus has done for us on the cross. It enables us to be in a relationship with God and to live a righteous life. We need to resist the devil. The apostle James says, "Resist the devil, and he will flee from you. Come near to God and he will come near to you" (James 4:7-8). We all fall from time to time. When we do, we need to get up quickly. We do this by telling God how sorry we are for what we have done, being as specific as possible (1 John 1:9). He then promises to restore His friendship with us.

Then, we also need the boots of the gospel of peace (v. 15). I understand this to mean a readiness to speak about the gospel of Jesus Christ. As John Wimber often said, "It is hard to sit still and be good." If we are constantly seeking opportunities to pass on the good news, we have an effective defense against the enemy. Once we declare our Christian faith to our families and at work, we strengthen our defense. It is hard, because we know that we are being watched to see if we live up to our faith. But it is a great incentive to do so.

The fourth piece of armor is the shield of faith (v. 16). With this, we "can extinguish all the flaming arrows of the evil one." Faith is the opposite of cynicism and skepticism, which wreak havoc in many lives. One aspect of faith has been defined as "taking a promise of God and daring to believe it." Satan will throw his arrows of doubt to undermine us—but with the shield of faith we resist him.

Fifth, Paul tells us to take the helmet of salvation (v. 17). As Bishop Westcott, former Regius Professor of Divinity at Cambridge University, once pointed out, there are three tenses of salvation. We have been saved from the penalty of sin. We are being saved from the power of sin. We shall be saved from the presence of sin. We need to grasp these great concepts in our mind, to know them so that we can answer the enemy's doubts and accusations.

Finally, we are to take "the sword of the Spirit, which is the word of God" (v. 17). Here Paul is thinking of the Scriptures. Jesus used the Scriptures when Satan attacked. Each time Jesus replied with the word of God and in the end Satan had to leave. It is well worth learning verses from the Bible, which we can use to send off the enemy and remind ourselves of the promises of God.

How do we attack?

As we have already seen, Satan was defeated on the cross, and we are now involved in the final mopping-up operations before the return of Jesus. As Christians, we need not be afraid of Satan; he has a great deal to fear from the activity of Christians.

We are called to pray: "And pray in the Spirit on all kinds of occasions with all kinds of prayers and requests" (v. 18). We are involved in spiritual warfare, though "the weapons we fight with are not the weapons of the world. On the contrary, they have divine power to demolish strongholds" (2 Corinthians 10:4). Prayer was a very high priority for Jesus, and it should be for us. In the words of the hymn, "Satan trembles when he sees the weakest Christian on his knees."

We are also called to action. Again, in the life of Jesus, prayer and action go hand in hand. Jesus proclaimed the kingdom of God, healed the sick, and cast out demons. He commissioned His disciples to do the same. Later on, we will look in more detail at what this means.

It is important to stress the greatness of God and the relative powerlessness of the enemy. We do not believe that there are two equal and opposite powers—God and Satan. That is not the biblical picture. God is the Creator of the universe. Satan is a part of His creation—a fallen part. He is a small part. Further, he is a defeated enemy and is about to be utterly wiped out when Jesus returns (Revelation 12:12).

In a superb picture in C. S. Lewis' book *The Great Divorce*, where he speaks about hell as the place where Satan and his demons operate, a man has arrived in heaven and is being shown round by his "teacher." He goes down on hands and knees, takes a blade of grass and, using the thin end as a pointer, he eventually finds a tiny crack in the soil in which is concealed the whole of hell:

> "Do you mean then that Hell—all that infinite empty town—is down in some little crack like this?"
>
> "Yes. All Hell is smaller than one pebble of your earthly world: but it is smaller than one atom of *this* world, the Real World. Look at yon butterfly. If it swallowed all Hell, Hell would not be big enough to do it any harm or to have any taste."
>
> "It seems big enough when you are in it, Sir."
>
> "And yet all loneliness, angers, hatreds, envies and itchings that it contains, if rolled into one single experience and put into the scale against the least moment of the joy that is felt by the least in Heaven, would have

no weight that could be registered at all. Bad cannot succeed even in being bad as truly as good is good. If all Hell's miseries together entered the consciousness of yon wee yellow bird on the bough there, they would be swallowed up without trace, as if one drop of ink had been dropped into that Great Ocean to which your terrestrial Pacific itself is only a molecule."[71]

CHAPTER 12

WHY AND HOW SHOULD I TELL OTHERS?

I used to be rather irritated by Christians who tried to tell me about their faith. My reaction was, "I am an atheist, but I don't go around trying to make atheists of other people." It seemed to me interfering.

"I happen to believe in chocolate, but I eat it
quietly, alone, in my own room"

Why should Christians talk about their faith? Isn't it a private matter? Isn't the best sort of Christian the one who just lives the Christian life? Sometimes people say to me, "I have a good friend who is a devout Christian. They have a really strong faith—but they do not talk about it. Isn't that the highest form of Christianity?"

The short answer is that someone must have told *them* about the Christian faith. If the early Christians hadn't told people about Jesus, none of us today would know about Him. The longer answer is that there are good reasons for telling others about Jesus. First, it is a command of Jesus Himself. Tom Forrest, the Roman Catholic priest who first suggested to the Pope the idea of calling the 1990s "The Decade of Evangelism," points out that the word "go" appears 1,514 times in the Bible (RSV), 233 times in the New Testament and 54 times in Matthew's Gospel. Jesus tells us to "go":

> *"Go to the lost sheep ..."*
> *"Go and tell ..."*
> *"Go and invite all you meet ..."*
> *"Go and make disciples ..."*

Indeed, these are the last recorded words of Jesus in Matthew's Gospel:

> Then Jesus came to them and said, "All authority in heaven and on earth has been given to me. Therefore go and make disciples of all nations, baptizing them in the name of the Father and of the Son and of the Holy Spirit, and teaching them to obey everything I have commanded you. And surely I will be with you always, to the very end of the age." (Matthew 28:18-20)

Second, we tell people because of our love for others. If we were in the Sahara Desert and had discovered an oasis, it would be extremely selfish not to tell the people around us who were thirsty where their thirst could be satisfied. Jesus is the only one who can satisfy the thirsty hearts of men and women. Often the recognition of this thirst comes from surprising sources. The singer, Sinead O'Connor, said in an interview, "As a race we feel empty. This is because our spirituality has been wiped out and we don't know how to express ourselves. As a result we're encouraged to fill that gap with alcohol, drugs, sex, or money. People out there are screaming for the truth."

Third, we tell others because, having discovered the good news ourselves, we feel an urgent desire to pass it on. If we have received good news we want to tell other people. When our first child was born, we had a list of about ten people to call first. Top of the list was Pippa's mother. I told her that we had a son and that he and Pippa were well. I then tried calling my mother, but the phone was busy. The third person on the list was Pippa's sister. By the time I had telephoned her she had already heard the news from Pippa's mother and so had all the others

"I know you're only a postbox, but you
need to know about Jesus"

on the list. My mother's phone had been busy because Pippa's mother was calling her with the news. Good news travels fast. I did not need to implore Pippa's mother to pass on the message. She was bursting to tell them all. When we are excited about our relationship with Jesus, it is the most natural thing in the world to want to tell people.

But how do we go about telling others? It seems to me that there are two opposite dangers. First, there is the danger of insensitivity. When I first became a Christian I fell into this. I was so excited about what had happened that I longed for everyone else to follow suit. After I had been a Christian for a few days, I went to a party determined to tell everyone. I saw a friend dancing and decided the first step was to make her realize her need for God. So I went up to her and said, "You look awful. You really need Jesus." She thought that I had gone mad. It was not the most effective way of telling someone the good news! (However, she did later become a Christian, quite independently of me, and she is now my wife!)

The next party I went to, I decided to go well equipped. I got hold of a number of booklets, Christian books on various issues and a New Testament. I stuffed them into every pocket I could find. Somehow I managed to find a girl who was willing to dance with me. It was hard with so many books in my pocket, so I asked if we could sit down. I soon brought the subject around to Christianity. For every question she asked, I was able to produce a book from my pocket on exactly that subject. Eventually she went away with an armful of books. The next day she was going to France and was reading one of the books I had given her on the boat. Suddenly she understood the truth of what Jesus had done for her and, turning to her neighbor, she said, "I have just become a Christian." Not much later, tragically, she died in a riding accident at the age of twenty-one. Even though I didn't go about it in quite the right way, it was wonderful that she had come to Christ before she died.

If we charge around like a bull in a china shop, sooner or later we get hurt. Even if we approach the subject sensitively, we may still get hurt. When we do, we tend to withdraw. Certainly this was my experience. After a few years, I moved from the danger of

insensitivity and fell into the opposite danger of fear. There was a time (ironically, it was when I was in seminary) when I became fearful of even talking about Jesus to those who were not Christians. On one occasion, a group of us went from the seminary to a parish mission on the outskirts of Liverpool, to tell people the good news. Each night we had supper with different people from the parish. One night, a friend of mine named Rupert and I were sent to supper with a couple who were on the fringe of the church (or, to be more accurate, the wife was on the fringe, and the husband was not a churchgoer). Halfway through the main course the husband asked me what we were doing up there. I stumbled, stammered, hesitated, and prevaricated. He kept on repeating the question. Eventually Rupert said straight out, "We have come here to tell people about Jesus." I felt deeply embarrassed and hoped the ground would swallow us all up! I realized how frozen with fear I had become, and that I was afraid to even utter the word "Jesus."

In order to avoid these dangers of insensitivity and fear, we need to realize that telling others about Jesus arises out of our own relationship with God. It is a natural part of that relationship. I find it helpful to think of this subject under five headings—all beginning with the letter "p": presence, persuasion, proclamation, power, and prayer.

Presence

Jesus said to His disciples:

> You are the salt of the earth. But if the salt loses its saltiness, how can it be made salty again? It is no longer good for anything, except to be thrown out and trampled by men. You are the light of the world. A city on a hill cannot be hidden. Neither do people light a lamp and put it under a bowl. Instead they put it on its stand, and it gives light to everyone in the house. In the same way, let your light shine before men, that they may see your good deeds and praise your Father in heaven. (Matthew 5:13-16)

Jesus calls us to have a wide-ranging influence ("salt of the *earth*" and "the light of the *world*"). In order to exercise this influence we need to be "in the world" (at work, where we live, and among our family and friends) and not withdrawn from it. Yet we are called to be different—to live as followers of Christ in the world, so that we can be effective as salt and light in it.

In the ancient world, without refrigeration, salt was used to keep meat wholesome and to prevent it from rotting. As Christians, we are called to stop society going bad. We do this, for example, as we speak out about moral and social issues and as we work to alleviate poverty and inequality.

Second, Jesus calls us to be light, and He reminds us that it's no good covering a lamp. How do we light up the world? By our good deeds, says Jesus: by everything we do as Christians.

Living out the Christian life is the most appropriate way of passing on the good news to those who live in very close proximity to us. This certainly applies to our family, work colleagues, and those we live with.

When I first became a Christian, I immediately tried to convert my parents. But I then realized that this was counter-productive. A friend pointed out that to declare to my parents, "I've become a Christian," was an implied criticism of how they had brought me up. Continually speaking about our faith may backfire. People are more likely to be affected by genuine love and concern—by living out the Christian faith. Similarly, at work people should notice our consistency, honesty, truthfulness, hard work, reliability, refusal to gossip, and desire to encourage other people.

This is of great importance if one's husband or wife is not a Christian. Peter encouraged Christian wives that if any of them have husbands who "do not believe the word, they may be won over *without words* by the behavior of their wives, when they see the purity and reverence of your lives" (1 Peter 3:1, italics mine).

Bruce and Geraldine Streather were married in December 1973. When Geraldine became a Christian in 1981, Bruce was not remotely interested. He was a busy lawyer and most weekends he used to play golf, rather than go to church.

For ten years Geraldine prayed for him and lived the Christian life at home as best she could. She did not put any pressure on him. Over the years, Bruce was struck by her kindness and consideration, especially to his mother whose cancer and related illnesses made their life increasingly difficult. Eventually, in 1991, she invited him to come to an Alpha supper. Bruce came, and decided to go on the following Alpha course.

Geraldine wrote to me afterwards saying, "I cried all the way home and prayed, telling God that as I had gotten Bruce to Alpha, He must do the rest. When Bruce returned from the first night of the course, all I asked him was whether he had enjoyed himself. On the seventh week of the course, Bruce gave his life to Christ and by the end he was one of the most enthusiastic Christians I have ever met." Her letter continued: "At every dinner party we go to he talks to people about God and I'm left at the other end of the table listening to what he is saying. It seems that all my prayers have been answered."

We are called to be salt and light, not just to our family and our immediate friends, but also to all the people around us. Sometimes we can struggle to see "beyond the narrow confines of our own little worlds." However, we are called to have compassion for those who are suffering. We can do this by getting involved in projects that relieve human need: hunger, homelessness, and poverty. We are also called to fight for social justice. We can do this by campaigning to abolish exploitation, inequality, and inhumanity.

William Wilberforce was twenty-seven when he sensed God's call to fight against the inhuman, degrading slave trade. Ten million slaves had left Africa for the plantations by 1787, and in that year he put down a motion in the House of Commons concerning the slave trade. It was not a popular cause, but he said this in his Abolition Speech: "So enormous, so dreadful did its wickedness appear that my own mind was completely made up for abolition. Let the consequences be what they would; I from that time determined I would never rest until I had effected its abolition."

Bills were debated in 1789, 1791, 1792, 1794, 1796, 1798 and 1799 and they all failed. In 1831 he sent a message to the Anti-Slavery Society in which he said: "Our motto must be perseverance, and ultimately I trust the Almighty will crown our efforts with success." In July 1833 the Abolition of Slavery Bill was passed in both Houses of Parliament. Three days later Wilberforce died. He was buried in Westminster Abbey in national recognition of his forty-five years of persevering struggle on behalf of African slaves.

There are issues today that are on the same scale. 1.3 billion individuals are trapped in absolute poverty, a condition characterized by malnutrition, disease, squalor, infant mortality, and low life expectancy. Eight hundred million people live on less than a dollar a day and go to bed hungry every night. Every three seconds, poverty takes a child's life. Every day, 30,000 children die of treatable diseases. Every day, 8,000 people die of AIDS in developing countries. There are 15 million preventable deaths each year and slavery remains an issue in many parts of the world.

Bono, lead singer of the Irish rock band U2, was invited to address the Labor Party Conference in 2004. He spoke about his time working in an Ethiopian orphanage:

> The locals knew me as "Dr. Good Morning." The children called me "The girl with a beard." Don't ask! It just blew my mind; it opened my mind. On our last day at the orphanage a man handed me his baby and said, "Take him with you." He knew in Ireland his son would live; in Ethiopia his son would die. I turned him down. In that moment I started this journey. In that moment I became the worst thing of all: a rock-star with a cause. Except this isn't a cause—6,500 Africans dying a day of treatable, preventable disease, dying for want of medicines you and I can get at our local chemist: that's not a cause; that's an emergency.

It is easy to be overwhelmed by the scale of these problems and to think, "Can we really make a difference?" Is there anything we can do as individuals?

One day a man was walking along a beach as the tide was receding. He saw tens of thousands of starfish stranded on the beach, drying out and slowly dying. He noticed a young boy picking up the starfish one at a time, and throwing them back into the sea. He approached the boy and said to him, "With tens of thousands of those starfish lying up and down the beach you must feel like you're not making much of a difference." As the boy tossed yet another starfish into the sea he turned to the man and said, "I bet it made a difference to that one."

In a similar way, we might not be able to solve all the problems in the world, but we can do something. Nelson Mandela said, "It's not the kings and generals who make history, but the masses of the people."

Having said this, being "lights in the world" does not just involve our lifestyle, it also involves our lips. Our family, friends, and colleagues will eventually ask questions about our faith. Peter writes: "Always be prepared to give an answer to everyone who asks you to give the reason for the hope that you have. But do this with gentleness and respect" (1 Peter 3:15).

When we do get opportunities to speak, how do we go about it?

Persuasion

Many people today have objections to the Christian faith or, at least, questions which they want answered before they are ready to come to faith in Christ. They need to be persuaded about the truth. Paul was willing to try to persuade people, because he loved them: "Since, then, we know what it is to fear the Lord, we try to *persuade* men" (2 Corinthians 5:11, italics mine).

There is a big difference between persuasion and pressure. I, for one, run a mile if anyone tries to pressure me to do anything. The effect of pressure is the opposite to that of persuasion. When Paul went to Thessalonica he "reasoned," "explained," and "proved" from the Scriptures that Christ had to suffer and rise from the dead: ". . . some of the Jews were persuaded . . ." (Acts 17:4). In Corinth, while making tents during the week, "every Sabbath he reasoned in the synagogue, trying to persuade Jews and Greeks" (Acts 18:4).

During the course of conversations about the Christian faith, objections will often be raised and we need to be equipped to deal with these. On one occasion, Jesus was talking to a woman about the mess her life was in (John 4). Then He offered her eternal life. At that moment she raised a theological question about places of worship. He answered it, but quickly brought the conversation back to the essential issue. This is a good example for us to follow.

As well as being prepared to give an answer, we must also be prepared to listen to people, to understand where they are coming from. When I was struggling with the Christian faith, I did have intellectual objections. However, I was also beginning to realize the implications that becoming a Christian might have for my lifestyle. I was even worried that, since I had argued quite publicly at university against Christianity; I would lose face if I suddenly announced that I had become a Christian. There can, therefore, be other factors at work to which we need to be sensitive.

I am very grateful to the people who did help me to overcome my objections. When the crew first realized that the Titanic was sinking, they rushed around trying to persuade people to get into the lifeboats, but many passengers didn't believe them and wouldn't get in. Some of those early lifeboats went away half-empty. Yet the crew were trying to persuade them to get in out of love. Similarly, trying to persuade people about Christianity is an act of love.

Proclamation

The heart of telling others is the proclamation of the good news of Jesus Christ. There are many ways in which this can be done.

1. Come and see

One of the simplest and most effective ways is bringing people to hear the gospel explained by someone else. This can often be more advisable, especially in the early stages of our Christian lives, than trying to explain the gospel ourselves.

Many who come to faith in Christ have lots of friends who have little or no connection with the church. This provides an excellent opportunity to say to these friends, as Jesus did on one occasion, "Come . . . and you will see" (John 1:39). A woman in her twenties became a Christian and started coming to church in London. On weekends, however, she would stay with her parents in Wiltshire, and then she insisted on leaving them at 3 P.M. on Sunday afternoon in order make it to church. One Sunday evening she got stuck in a bad traffic jam on the way into London and could not get to the evening service. She was so upset that she burst into tears. She went to see some friends, who did not even know she had become a Christian. They asked her what was wrong. She answered through the tears, "I've missed church." They were totally mystified. The next Sunday they all came to see what they were missing! One of them became a Christian soon afterwards.

There is no higher privilege and no greater joy than enabling someone to find out about Jesus Christ. The former Archbishop of Canterbury, William Temple, wrote a commentary on John's Gospel. When he came to the words, "And he [Andrew] brought Simon to Jesus," he wrote a short but momentous sentence: "The greatest service that one man can render another."

We don't hear much more about Andrew except that he was always bringing people to Jesus (John 6:8; 12:22). But Simon Peter, his brother, went on to be one of the greatest influences in the history of Christianity. We cannot all be Simon Peters, but we can all do what Andrew did—we can bring someone to Jesus.

Albert McMakin was a twenty-four-year-old farmer who had recently come to faith in Christ. He was so full of enthusiasm that he filled a van with people and took them to a meeting to hear about Jesus. There was a good-looking farmer's son whom he was especially keen to get to a meeting, but this young man was hard to persuade—he was busy falling in and out of love with different girls, and did not seem to be attracted to Christianity. Eventually, Albert McMakin managed to persuade him to come by asking him to drive the van. When they arrived, Albert's guest decided to go in, was "spellbound" and began to have thoughts he had never known before. He went back again and again until one night, he went forward and gave his life to Jesus Christ. That man, the driver of the van, was Billy Graham. The year was 1934. Since then Billy Graham has spoken to 210 million people in person about the Christian faith. He has been the friend and confidant of nine American presidents. We cannot all be like Billy Graham, but we can all do what Albert McMakin did—we can all bring our friends to Jesus.

2. Tell our own story

One powerful way of communicating the gospel is to tell our own story. We see a biblical model in Paul's testimony in Acts 26:9-23. It falls into three parts: he speaks about what he was like before (vv. 9-11), what it meant to meet Jesus (vv. 12-15), and what it has meant for him since (vv. 19-23).

When a blind man was healed by Jesus, many people came to question him about it, including the Pharisees who cross-examined him and tried to trap him. The blind man did not know how to answer all their questions but he knew what God had done: "One thing I do know. I was blind but now I see!" (John 9:25). It is hard to argue with that.

3. Explain the gospel yourself

When explaining what someone has to do to become a Christian, a framework can be helpful. There are many different ways of presenting the gospel. I have set out the method I use in a booklet called *Why Jesus?* I then lead people in the prayer which you will find at the end of chapter 4 of this book.

One man in our church told me about how he had come to Christ. He was going through difficulties in his business and had to go to the United States on a business trip. He was not feeling very happy as he rode in a taxi to the airport. On the dashboard of the taxi he noticed pictures of the taxi driver's children, so he asked him about his family. As they went on, he felt great love coming from the man. As the conversation went on, the taxi driver said to him, "I sense that you are not happy. If you believe in Christ it makes all the difference."

The businessman said to me, "Here was a man speaking with authority. I thought I was the one in authority. After all, I was paying." The taxi driver said to him eventually, "Don't you think it's time you settled all this by accepting Christ?" When they arrived at the airport, the taxi driver said to him, "Why don't we pray? If you want Christ in your life, ask Him." They prayed together. That moment changed the whole course of a man's life.

Power

In the New Testament the proclamation of the gospel is often accompanied by a demonstration of the power of God. Jesus came proclaiming: "The kingdom of God is near. Repent and believe the good news!" (Mark 1:15). Jesus went on to demonstrate the power of the gospel by the expulsion of evil (Mark 1:21-28) and by healing the sick (Mark 1:29-34, 40-45).

Jesus told His disciples to do what He had been doing. He told them to do the works of the kingdom—"to heal the sick who are there" and to proclaim the good news—and to tell them, "The kingdom of God is near you" (Luke 10:9). As we read on in the Gospels and Acts we see that this is what they did. Paul wrote to the Thessalonians: "Our gospel came to you not simply with words, but also with power" (1 Thessalonians 1:5). This was certainly true for me; when I first encountered the power of the Holy Spirit, I experienced what Paul speaks of in Romans 5:5: "The love of God has been poured out in our hearts by the Holy Spirit who was given to us" (NKJV). Other people testify to the experience of being overwhelmed by the power of the Holy Spirit in terms of the conviction of their sin. When they hear the good news about Jesus, something deeper is going on in their hearts.

Proclamation and demonstration go hand in hand. One often leads to the other. On one occasion Peter and John were on their way to church. Outside was a man crippled from birth. He had been sitting there for years. He asked for money. Peter said, in effect, "I am sorry. I haven't got any money, but I will give you what I have. In the name of Jesus Christ of Nazareth, walk" He took his hand and helped him up. Instantly, he jumped to his feet and began to walk. When he realized he was healed, he leapt and jumped and praised God (Acts 3:1-10).

Everyone knew that this man had been crippled for years, and a huge crowd gathered around. After the demonstration of the power of God came the proclamation of the gospel. People were asking, "How did this happen?" Peter was able to tell them all about Jesus: "It is Jesus' name and the faith that comes through him that has given this complete healing to him, as you can all see" (Acts 3:16). In the next chapter we shall examine this area in more detail by looking at the nature of the kingdom of God and the place of healing within it.

Prayer

We have already seen the importance that prayer had in the life of Jesus. While He was proclaiming and demonstrating the gospel He was also praying (Mark 1:35-37). Prayer is essential in the area of telling others the good news. Similarly, Paul loved people, and out of that love came a desire to pray for them, "My heart's desire and prayer to God . . . is that they may be saved" (Romans 10:1).

We need to pray for blind eyes to be opened. Many people are blinded to the gospel (2 Corinthians 4:4). They can see physically, but they cannot see the spiritual world. We need to pray that the Spirit of God will open the eyes of the blind so that they can understand the truth about Jesus.

Most of us find, when we come to faith in Christ, that there has been somebody praying for us. It may be a member of the family, a godparent, or a friend. When a friend of mine, Ric, became a Christian he called a friend whom he knew to be a Christian as well, and told him what had happened. The friend replied, "I have been praying for you for four years." Ric then started to pray for one of his own friends, and within ten weeks he too became a Christian.

We need to pray for our friends. We also need to pray for ourselves. When we talk to people about Jesus, we may sometimes get a negative reaction. The temptation at that moment is to give up. When Peter and John healed the crippled man and proclaimed the gospel, they were arrested and threatened with dire consequences should they continue. But they did not give up. Rather, they prayed—for boldness in preaching the gospel and for God to perform more signs and wonders through the name of Jesus (Acts 4:29-31).

It is vital for all of us as Christians to persevere in telling others about Jesus—by our presence, persuasion, proclamation, power, and prayer. If we do, over the course of a lifetime we shall see many lives changed.

During the war a man was shot and lay dying in the trenches. A friend leaned over to him and said, "Is there anything I can do for you?"

He replied, "No, I am dying."

"Is there anyone I can send a message to for you?"

"Yes, you can send a message to this man at this address. Tell him that in my last minutes what he taught me as a child is helping me to die."

The man was his old Sunday school teacher. When the message got back to him, he said, "God forgive me. I gave up Sunday school teaching years ago because I thought I was getting nowhere. I thought it was no use."

When we tell people about Jesus, it is never "no use." For the gospel "is the power of God for the salvation of everyone who believes" (Romans 1:16).

CHAPTER 13

DOES GOD HEAL TODAY?

A few years ago, a Japanese girl asked Pippa and me to pray for her back problem to be healed. We placed our hands on her and asked God to heal her. After that I tried to avoid bumping into her because I was not sure how to explain to her why she hadn't been healed. One day she came round the corner and I could not avoid her. I thought it only polite to ask the dreaded question, "How is your back?"

"Oh," she replied, "it was completely healed after you prayed for it."

I don't know why I was so surprised, but I was.

In 1982, John Wimber came to speak at our church. At the time I was practicing as a barrister. I was quite cynical about his visit because, not only had he come from California to speak about healing, but he also wanted us to "do healing." Although I had heard some talks on healing before, no one had ever suggested that we actually try it. This was unfamiliar territory. After giving his talk to a gathering of sixty leaders from the church he announced that we were going to break for coffee, before having a workshop.

We were nervous about this prospect and dragged out the coffee break for as long as we could. When we returned, the people who had been at the front felt it would be selfish to hog the best seats, so they hurried to the back! John then said that his team had received twelve "words of knowledge" about people in the room. He told us that by a "word of knowledge" (1 Corinthians 12:8) he meant a supernatural revelation of facts concerning a person or a situation, which is not learned by the efforts of the natural mind, but rather is made known by the Spirit of God. This could be in the form of a picture, a word seen or heard in the mind, or a feeling experienced physically. He then read out the list of words of knowledge and said that he was going to invite people to come forward for prayer.

One by one, people responded to what were quite detailed descriptions. One word, for instance, was for a man who had injured his back chopping wood when he was aged fourteen. The level of faith in the room began to rise. Every word of knowledge was responded to. One of them concerned infertility. Being British we don't even talk about subjects like that, let alone respond to "words of knowledge" about them. However, a girl who had been unable to conceive bravely went forward. She was prayed for and had the first of five children exactly nine months later!

My attitude during that evening reflects the fear and skepticism that many bring to the subject of healing today. I decided to go back to the Bible to try to understand what is said about healing. Of course, God heals with the co-operation of doctors, nurses, and the medical profession. But the more I have looked, the more convinced I am that we should also expect God to heal miraculously today.

Healing in the Bible

In the Old Testament we find that it is in God's character to heal, "I am the Lord, who heals you" (Exodus 15:26). We find God's promises to bring healing to those who listen to Him and who honor Him (e.g., Exodus 23:25-26; Psalm 41), as well as several examples of miraculous healing (e.g., 1 Kings 13:6; 2 Kings 4:8-37; Isaiah 38).

One of the most striking examples is the healing of Naaman, the commander of the army of Aram, who had leprosy. God healed him after he had reluctantly dipped himself seven times in the River Jordan. "His flesh was restored and became clean like that of a young boy" (2 Kings 5:14), and he recognized the God of Israel to be the only true God. Elisha, who had instructed him, refused the payment, which Naaman offered (although his servant Gehazi made the fatal mistake of trying, deceitfully, to get money for himself as a result of the healing). First, from this story we see that healing can have a remarkable effect on a person's life—not just physically, but also in their relationship with God. Healing and faith can go hand in hand. Secondly, if God acted in this way in the Old Testament, when there were only glimpses of the kingdom of God and the outpouring of the Spirit, we can confidently expect that He will do so even more now that Jesus has ushered in the kingdom of God and the age of the Spirit.

The first recorded words of Jesus in Mark's Gospel are, "The time has come . . . The kingdom of God is near. Repent and believe the good news!" (Mark 1:15). The theme of the kingdom of God is central to the ministry of Jesus. The expressions "the kingdom of God" and "the kingdom of heaven" are used more than eighty-two times, although the latter is confined to Matthew's Gospel.[72] The Greek word for "kingdom," means not only "kingdom" in the sense of a political or geographical realm, but also carries the notion of activity—the activity of ruling or reigning.

In the teaching of Jesus, the kingdom of God has a future aspect that will only be fulfilled with a decisive event at "the end of the age" (Matthew 13:49). The end of the age will come when Jesus returns. When He came the first time, He came in weakness; when He returns, He will come "with power and great glory" (Matthew 24:30). History is moving towards this climax (Matthew 25:31). In all, there are over 300 references in the New Testament to the second coming of Christ. When He returns it will be obvious to all. History, as we know it, will end. There will be a universal resurrection and a Day of Judgment (2 Thessalonians 1:8-9; Matthew 25:32). For some (those who reject Christ), it will be a day of destruction (2 Thessalonians 1:8-9); for others, it will be a day of receiving their inheritance in the kingdom of God (Matthew 25:34). There will be a new heaven and a new earth (2 Peter 3:13; Revelation 21:1). Jesus Himself will be there (Revelation 21:22-23) and so will all who love and obey Him. It will be a place of intense happiness which goes on for ever (1 Corinthians 2:9). We will have new bodies which are imperishable and glorious (1 Corinthians 15:42-43). There will be no more death or mourning or crying or pain (Revelation 21:4). All who believe will be totally healed on that day.

Until that day there is an element of waiting. As Paul puts it, "We . . . groan inwardly as we wait eagerly for . . . the redemption of our bodies" (Romans 8:23). That is, we wait eagerly for the age to come, when God will be "all in all" (1 Corinthians 15:28). It's important to keep this eternal perspective as we look at this subject, because at the moment not everybody is healed.

A good friend of mine, Patrick Pearson-Miles, has not been healed. He has kidney failure and has been on a dialysis machine for over fifteen years. He is a remarkably brave man, and also a man of great faith. He has been praying for healing for many years, and we have prayed for him many times, but so far he has not been healed. Patrick said how much he was helped by a conversation he had with John Wimber, who himself suffered with cancer for many years. John said to him, "The real gift is that of salvation, eternal life, all the things that Jesus gives us. If we're healed physically in this life that, if you like, is a bonus." It's vital to keep in mind this future aspect of God's kingdom.

There is also a present aspect to the kingdom as we see in the teaching and life of Jesus. He told the Pharisees, "The kingdom of God is within you" (Luke 17:20-21). It's for the here and now: the signs of its approach are evident to us. In the parables of the hidden treasure and the pearl of great price (Matthew 13:44-46), Jesus suggests that the kingdom is something which can be discovered and experienced in this age. He went on to demonstrate this present reality of the kingdom by all that He did during His ministry, in the forgiveness of sins, the suppression of evil, and the healing of the sick.

The kingdom is both "now" and "not yet." The Jewish expectation was that the Messiah would immediately inaugurate the final kingdom, as shown in the diagram below:

THIS AGE	**AGE TO COME**

Jesus' teaching was a modification of this and can be summarized in the diagram below:

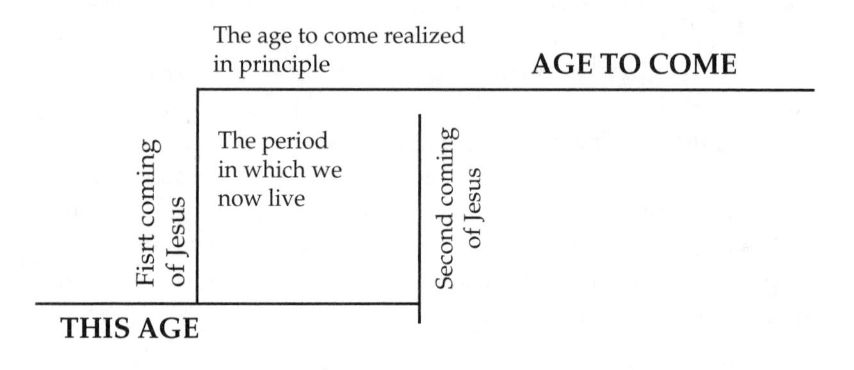

We live between the times, when the age to come has broken into history. We see people's bodies being healed and people being set free from addictions. But the old age continues, and the powers of the new age have erupted into this age.

A quarter of the Gospels is concerned with healing. Although Jesus did not heal all in Judea who were sick, we often read of Him healing either individuals, or groups of people (e.g., Matthew 4:23; 9:35; Mark 6:56; Luke 4:40; 6:19; 9:11). It was part of the normal activity of the kingdom.

Jesus preached the good news of the kingdom and healed the sick. Then He sent the twelve apostles out to do exactly the same. Jesus said to them, "Preach this message: 'The kingdom of heaven is near.' Heal the sick, raise the dead, cleanse those who have leprosy, drive out demons . . ." (Matthew 10:7-8).

Nor was it only the twelve to whom He gave this commission. There was also a further group of seventy-two whom He appointed. He told them to go out and "heal the sick . . . and tell them, 'The kingdom of God is near you'" (Luke 10:9). They returned with joy and said, "Lord, even the demons submit to us in your name" (v. 17).

Nor did He stop at the twelve and the seventy-two. Jesus expected *all* His disciples to do the same. He told His disciples to "go and make disciples of all nations . . . teaching them to obey *everything* I have commanded you" (Matthew 28:18-20, italics mine). He did not say, "Everything except, of course, the healing bit."

Furthermore, as you look at the development of the church in the New Testament you see this is what they did. In the Book of Acts we see the working out of this commission. The disciples continued to preach and teach, but they also healed the sick, raised the dead, and cast out demons. They didn't just talk about it; they did it! (Acts 3:1-10; 4:12; 5:12-16; 8:5-13; 9:32-43; 14:3, 8-10; 19:11-12; 20:9-12; 28:8-9). It is clear from 1 Corinthians 12–14 that Paul did not believe that such abilities were confined to the apostles. Likewise, the writer to the Hebrews says that God testified to His message by "signs, wonders and various miracles, and gifts of the Holy Spirit" (Hebrews 2:4).

Nowhere in the Bible does it suggest that healing was confined to any particular period of history. On the contrary, healing is one of the signs of the kingdom which was inaugurated by Jesus Christ and continues to this day. Therefore, we should expect God to continue to heal miraculously today as part of His kingdom activity.

Healing in church history

Early church writers such as Quadratus, Justin Martyr, Theophilus of Antioch, Irenaeus, Tertullian and Origen reveal that healing formed a normal part of the activity of the early church.

Irenaeus (c.130–c.200), who was Bishop of Lyons and one of the theologians of the early church, wrote, "Others still, heal the sick by laying their hands upon them, and they are made whole."

At around the same time, Origen (c.185–c.254), another early church father, said of Christians, "They expel evil spirits, and perform many cures, and foresee certain events . . . the name of Jesus . . . can take away diseases."

Two hundred years later there was still an expectation that God would heal people directly. St. Augustine wrote in *The City of God*, that "*even now* miracles are wrought in the name of Christ." He cites the example of a blind man's sight restored in Milan. He then describes the cure of a man he was staying with, named Innocentius. He was being treated by the doctors for fistulae, of which he had "a large number intricately seated in the rectum!" He had undergone one very painful operation. It was thought that he would not survive another. While they were praying for him he was cast down to the ground as if someone had hurled him violently to the earth, groaning and sobbing, his whole body shaking so that he could not speak. The dreaded day for the next operation came. "The surgeons arrived . . . the frightful instruments are produced . . . the part is bared; the surgeon . . . with knife in hand, eagerly looks for the sinus that is to be cut. He searches for it with his eyes; he feels for it with his finger; he applies every kind of scrutiny." He found a perfectly healed wound. "No words of mine can describe the joy, and praise, and thanksgiving to the merciful and almighty God which was poured from the lips of all, with tears and gladness. Let the scene be imagined rather than described!"

Next he described the healing of Innocentia—a devout woman of the highest rank in the state—who was healed of what the doctors described as incurable breast cancer. The doctor was curious to find out how she had been healed. When she told him that Jesus had healed her, he was furious and said, "I thought you would make some great discovery to me." She, shuddering at the indifference, quickly replied, "What great thing was it for Christ to heal a cancer, who raised one who had been four days dead?"

He goes on to tell of a doctor with gout who was healed in the "very act of baptism" and an old comedian who was also cured at baptism, not only of paralysis, but also of a hernia. Augustine says he knows of so many miraculous healings that he says at one point, "What am I to do? I am so pressed by the promise of finishing this work, that I cannot record all the miracles I know . . . even now, therefore many miracles are wrought, the same God, who wrought those we read of, still performing them, by whom he will and as he will."

Edward Gibbon, the English rationalist, historian and scholar, best known as the author of *The History of the Decline and Fall of the Roman Empire* (1776–1788), lists five causes for the remarkable and rapid growth of Christianity. One of these is "the miraculous powers of the primitive Church." He says, "The Christian Church, from the time of the apostles and their first disciples has claimed an uninterrupted succession of miraculous powers, the gift of tongues, of vision and of prophecy, the power of expelling demons, of healing the sick and of raising the dead." Gibbon goes on to point out the inconsistency of his own day when "a latent, and even involuntary, skepticism adheres to the most pious dispositions." By contrast to the early church, he writes that in the church of his day "admission of supernatural truths is much less an active consent than a cold and placid acquiescence. Accustomed long since to observe and to respect the invariable order of Nature, our reason, or at least our imagination, is not sufficiently prepared to sustain the visible action of the Deity." The same could be said even more so of our own day. All the way through church history God has continued to heal people directly.

Healing today

Some people believe that God chose to confine miraculous healing to the age of the early church. But God is still healing people today. In fact, there are so many wonderful stories of God healing that it is difficult to know which to give as an example.

I once met a woman named Jean Smith, who was then in her sixties. Sixteen and a half years previously she had an infection that had irrevocably eaten away the retinas and mirrors behind her eyes, and left her blind. As well as having to rely on a guide dog, she was also in a lot of pain. She had attended an Alpha course in her local church in Wales. On the weekend away she experienced the power of the Holy Spirit in a way she never had before. Amazingly, the pain she had suffered for so many years simply stopped. She went to church that evening to give thanks to God. The minister of her church then offered to anoint her with oil to signify this healing that had taken place over the weekend (in accordance with biblical practice). Wiping away the oil, she looked up, and she could see the communion table in front of her. She went home that night and saw her husband for the first time in sixteen and a half years. She could not believe how white his hair had gone!

Raniero Cantalamessa points out that Christians "have two ways to face up to our problems, and particularly to the problem of ill health: the way of nature and the way of grace."

> Human nature encompasses science and technology and all our resources: in short, all that we have received from God in creation and all that we have developed from that by using our intelligence. But then there's this second way: grace, which indicates faith and the prayers by which, as God may will, we sometimes obtain healings in a way that goes beyond the scope of human resources. Against disease and ill-health, a Christian cannot be satisfied to use only the facilities of "nature": to set up hospitals or to work along with the structures of the state to provide care and comfort. Christians have a very special power of their own, given to them by Christ: "[he] gave them authority ... to cure every disease and every sickness" (Matthew 10:1). It would be a sin of omission to fail to have recourse to this power and so fail to hold out hope to those to whom science denies all hope.[73]

Of course, not everyone we pray for will necessarily be healed, and no human being can ultimately avoid death. Our bodies are decaying. At some point it may even be right to prepare a person for death rather than praying for their healing. Indeed, the love and concern shown to people who are dying, for example, by the hospice movement, gives dignity to the terminally ill and is another outworking of Jesus' commission to care for the sick. At this point we need to be sensitive to the guidance of the Holy Spirit.

We should still be open to praying for people to be healed. The more people we pray for, the more we shall see healed.[74] Those who are not healed usually speak of the blessing of being prayed for—provided they are prayed for with love and sensitivity. I remember a group of us at seminary praying for a man with a bad back. I don't think he was healed, but he said to me afterwards, "This is the first time since I have been at seminary that I felt anyone cared."

Some are given special gifts of healing (1 Corinthians 12:9). Today, around the world, we find examples of those with an extraordinary gift of healing. This does not mean that we can leave it all to them. The commission to heal is for all of us. Just as we do not all have the gift of being evangelists, but we are all called to tell others the good news, so too we do not all have the gift of healing, but we are all called to pray for the sick.

How, in practice, do we go about praying for the sick? It is vital to remember that it is God who heals, not us. There is no technique involved. We pray with love and simplicity. The motivation of Jesus was His compassion for people (Mark 1:41; Matthew 9:36). If we love people we will always treat them with respect and dignity. If we believe it is Jesus who heals we will pray with simplicity, because it is not our prayer, but the power of God that brings healing.

Here is a simple pattern:

Where does it hurt?

We ask the person who wants prayer for healing what is wrong and what they would like us to pray for.

Why does the person have this condition?

Of course, a leg broken in a car accident will be obvious, but at other times we may need to ask God to show us if there is a root cause to the problem. One woman in our congregation had developed backache with pain in her left hip, which interfered with sleep, movement, and work. The doctor prescribed pills for arthritis. She asked for prayer one evening. The girl who was praying for her said that the word "forgiveness" had come to her mind. After a struggle the woman was able to forgive somebody who had wronged her, and she was partially healed. Later, as she prayed with someone else, she felt she ought to write the person a letter telling them that she forgave them. As she mailed the letter she was totally healed.

How do I pray?

There are various models in the New Testament that we follow. They are all simple. Sometimes we pray for God to heal in the name of Jesus and we ask the Holy Spirit to come on the person. Prayer may be accompanied by anointing with oil (James 5:14). More often it is accompanied by the laying on of hands (Luke 4:40).

How are they feeling?

After we have prayed we usually ask the person what they are experiencing. Sometimes they feel nothing—in which case we continue to pray. At other times they feel that they are healed, although time alone will tell. On other occasions they feel better but are not totally healed, in which case we continue as Jesus did with the blind man (Mark 8:22-25). We continue praying until we feel it is right to stop.

What next?

After praying for healing it is important to reassure people of God's love for them regardless of whether they are healed or not, and to give them the liberty to come back and be prayed for again. We must avoid putting burdens on people, such as suggesting that it is their lack of faith that has prevented healing from taking place. We always encourage people to go on praying and to ensure that their lives are rooted in the healing community of the church—which is the place where long-term healing so often occurs.

Finally, it is important to persist in praying for people to be healed. It is easy to get discouraged, especially if we do not see immediate dramatic results. We continue to pray out of obedience to Jesus' commission to preach the kingdom and heal the sick. If we persist, over the years we will see God's healing power at work.

I was once asked to visit a woman in the Brompton Hospital.

She was in her thirties, had three children and was pregnant with a fourth. Her partner had left her and she was on her own. Her third child, who had Down's syndrome, had a hole in his heart which had been operated on. The operation had not been a success and, not unnaturally, the medical staff wanted to turn the machines off. Three times they asked her if they could turn the machines off and let the baby die. She said no, as she wanted to try one last thing. She wanted someone to pray for him. So I came, and she told me that she didn't believe in God, but she showed me her son. He had tubes all over him and his body was bruised and swollen. She said that the doctors had indicated that even if he recovered he would have brain damage because his heart had stopped for such a long time. She said, "Will you pray?" So I prayed in the name of Jesus for God to heal him. Then I explained to her how she could give her life to Jesus Christ and she did that. I left, but returned two days later. She came running out the moment she saw me. She said, "I've been trying to get hold of you: something amazing has happened. The night after you prayed he completely turned the corner. He has recovered." Within a few days he had gone home. I tried to keep in contact with her, but didn't know where she lived, although she kept leaving messages on the phone. About six months later I was in the elevator in another hospital and saw a mother and child whom I did not immediately recognize. The woman said, "Are you Nicky?" I said, "Yes." She said, "That is the little boy you prayed for. It is amazing. Not only has he recovered from the operation, but his hearing, which was bad beforehand, is better."

Since then I have presided at two funerals for other members of that family. At each of them people have come up to me, none of them churchgoers, saying, "You were the person who prayed for Craig to be healed, and God healed him." They all believe that God healed him, because they know that he was dying. The change in Vivienne, the child's mother, had also made a deep impression on them. She was so changed after coming to Christ that she decided to marry the person with whom she was living. He had come back to her after seeing the change in her life. They are now married and she is totally transformed. On the second occasion, Vivienne went round to all the relatives and friends saying, "I didn't believe, but now I do believe."

Not long afterwards, Craig's uncle and aunt came to church, sat in the front row and gave their lives to Jesus Christ. They did so because they knew they had seen God's power in healing.

CHAPTER 14

WHAT ABOUT THE CHURCH?

Abraham Lincoln once said, "If all the people who fell asleep in church on Sunday morning were laid out end to end . . . they would be a great deal more comfortable." Before I became a Christian my heart used to sink when I heard the word "church." The first thing that came to mind was church services: hard pews, unsingable tunes, enforced silences, and excruciating boredom. A vicar was taking a small boy around his church one day and showing him the memorials. "These are the names of those who died in the Services." The boy asked, "Did they die at the morning service or at the evening service?"

Some associate the word "church" with the clergy. Someone who is entering the ordained ministry is said to be "going into the church." Those embarking on such a career are often viewed with suspicion, and the assumption is made that they are absolutely incapable of doing anything else. Hence a recent advertisement it the church press: "Are you forty-five and going nowhere? Why not consider the Christian ministry?" Clergy are sometimes perceived as: "Six days invisible, one day incomprehensible!"

Others associate the word "church" with denominations. My mother, before she became a Christian, filled out a form that asked for her religion. She replied, "None (Church of England)!" Still others associate "church" with buildings. They assume that to be a clergyman you must be interested in church architecture, and when they go on holiday they send their vicar a picture of the local church building.

There may be an element of truth in some of these views. Yet these associations don't capture the essence of the church. It is similar to asking, "What is marriage?" and receiving the answer that marriage is a ring, a marriage certificate, a wedding service, and the marriage laws. Marriage may involve all of those things, but they are not the essence. At the heart of marriage is something far more profound—a relationship of trust based upon love and commitment. Similarly, at the heart of the church is something beautiful—the relationship between God and his people. Over the years since I have been a Christian, I have come not just to like the church but to love it.

In the New Testament there are over 100 images or analogies of the church. In this chapter I want to look at five, which are central to our understanding of the church.

The people of God

First, the church is people. The Greek word for church, *ekklesia*, means "an assembly" or "gathering of people." The Christian faith involves first of all a vertical relationship (our relationship with God) but also a horizontal relationship (our relationship with other people). We are part of a community that began with God's call to Abraham; the people of Israel prefigured the church. So the universal church consists of all those across the world and down the ages who profess or have professed the name of Christ.

Baptism is a visible mark of being a member of the church. It is also a visible sign of what it means to be a Christian. It signifies cleansing from sin (1 Corinthians 6:11), dying and rising with Christ to a new life (Romans 6:3-5; Colossians 2:12), and the living water which the Holy Spirit brings to our lives (1 Corinthians 12:13). Jesus Himself commanded His followers to go and make disciples and to baptize them (Matthew 28:19).

The universal Christian church is vast. According to the

Encyclopaedia Britannica there are over two billion Christians in the world today, about a third of the world's population. Tens of thousands of people become Christians every day. Living in Western Europe, where the church has been in decline for many years, it is easy to think that the church is dying out. At one time, the West was sending missionaries out to other parts of the world. However, I remember that when I was in Cambridge, three Ugandan missionaries came there to preach the gospel. It struck me then how much the world had changed in the last 150 years, and that England needed missionaries as much as anywhere else.

Globally, the church is growing faster than ever. In 1900 there were 10 million Christians in Africa. One hundred years later there were 360 million. The same growth is evident in South America, China, and in various other parts of the world. In America about 50 per cent of the population goes to church on Sunday, compared with 7 per cent in the U.K.

In more than sixty countries in the world the church is persecuted. More than 200 million Christians are harassed, abused, tortured, or executed on account of their faith, living in daily fear of secret police, vigilantes, or state repression and discrimination.[75] Yet the church in those parts of the world, by all accounts, remains very strong.

In the New Testament, Paul speaks of local churches, for example the "Galatian churches" (1 Corinthians 16:1), "the churches in the province of Asia" (1 Corinthians 16:19), and "all the churches of Christ" (Romans 16:16). Even those local churches themselves seem at times to have broken down into smaller gatherings which met in homes (Romans 16:5; 1 Corinthians 16:19).

In effect, there seem to have been three types of gathering in the Bible: the large, the medium-sized, and the small. These have been described as "celebration," "congregation," and "cell." In our experience as a local church all three are important and complement each other.

The celebration is a large gathering of Christians. This may take place every Sunday in big churches, or when a number of small churches come together for worship. In the Old Testament, the people of God came together for special celebrations with a festive atmosphere at Passover, Pentecost, or at the New Year. Today, large gatherings of

Christians provide inspiration. Through them, many can recapture a vision of the greatness of God and a profound sense of worship. These gatherings of hundreds of Christians together can restore confidence to those who have felt isolated and provide a visible presence of the church in the community. However, on their own such gatherings are not enough. They are not places where friendships can easily develop.

The congregation, in this sense, is a medium-sized gathering. The size makes it possible to know most people. It is a place where lasting Christian friendships can be made. It is a place where individuals can learn, for example, to give talks, participate in worship, pray for the sick, participate in the liturgy and learn to pray out loud. It is also a place where the gifts and ministries of the Spirit, such as prophecy, can be exercised in an atmosphere of love and acceptance, where people are free to risk making mistakes. It is at this level that we can also go out as a group and serve our community. This could involve, for example, visiting the sick and elderly, painting the home of someone in need, or helping out at a homeless shelter or youth group.

The third level of meeting is the cell or small group. These groups consist of between two and twelve people, who gather to study the Bible and pray together. It is in these groups that the closest friendships in church are made. People are free to talk about their doubts, fears, and failures. We can encourage each other, eat together, and celebrate life's blessings. We can ask others to pray for us and be there for each other in difficult times. It should be a place of confidentiality, accountability, and respect.

The family of God

Second, the church is the family of God. When we receive Jesus Christ into our lives, we become children of God (John 1:12). This is what gives the church its unity. We have God as our Father, Jesus Christ as our Savior, and the Holy Spirit who lives within us. We all belong to one family. Although brothers and sisters may squabble and fall out or not see each other for long periods of time, they still remain brothers and sisters. Nothing can end that relationship. The church is one, even though it often appears to be divided.

This does not mean that we settle for disunity. Jesus prayed for His followers "that they may be one" (John 17:11). Paul says, "Make every effort to keep the unity of the Spirit" (Ephesians 4:3). Like a divided family we should always strive for reconciliation; our divisions are inevitably off-putting to those outside the church. Of course, unity should not be achieved at the expense of truth but, as the medieval writer Rupertus Meldenius put it, "On the necessary points, unity; on the questionable points, liberty; in everything, love."

At every level we should seek unity—in the small group, congregation, and celebration, and within our denomination and between denominations. This unity is brought about as theologians and church leaders get together to debate and work through theological differences. But it is also achieved, often more effectively, by ordinary Christians getting together to pray, worship, and work together. The nearer we come to Christ, the nearer we come to each other. David Watson, the writer and church leader, used a striking illustration. He said:

> When you travel by air and the plane lifts off the ground, the walls and hedges which may seem large and impressive at ground level, at once lose their significance. In the same way, when the power of the Holy Spirit lifts us up together into the conscious realization of the presence of Jesus, the barriers between us become unimportant. Seated with Christ in the heavenly places, the differences between Christians can often seem petty and marginal.[76]

Since we have the same Father, we are brothers and sisters and are all called to love one another. John puts it very clearly:

> If anyone says, "I love God," yet hates his brother, he is a liar. For anyone who does not love his brother, whom he has seen, cannot love God, whom he has not seen. And he has given us this command: Whoever loves God must also love his brother. Everyone who believes that Jesus is the Christ is born of God, and everyone who loves the father loves his child as well. (1 John 4:20–5:1)

Raniero Cantalamessa, addressing a gathering of thousands from many different denominations, said, "When Christians quarrel we say to God: 'Choose between us and them.' But the Father loves all

His children. We should say, 'We accept as our brothers and sisters all those whom You receive as Your children.'"

We are called to fellowship with one another. The Greek word *koinonia* means "having in common" or "sharing." It is the word used for the marital relationship, the most intimate between human beings. Our fellowship is with God (Father, Son, and Holy Spirit—1 John 1:3; 2 Corinthians 13:14) and with one another (1 John 1:7). Christian fellowship cuts across race, color, education, background, and every other cultural barrier. There is a level of friendship in the church which I have certainly never experienced outside the church.

John Wesley said, "The New Testament knows nothing of solitary religion." We are called to fellowship with one another. It is not an optional extra. There are two things we simply cannot do alone. We cannot marry alone and we cannot be a Christian alone. Professor C. E. B. Cranfield put it like this, "The freelance Christian, who would be a Christian but is too superior to belong to the visible Church upon earth in one of its forms, is simply a contradiction in terms."

The writer of Hebrews urges his readers, "Let us consider how we may spur one another on towards love and good deeds. Let us not give up meeting together, as some are in the habit of doing, but let us encourage one another—and all the more as you see the Day approaching" (Hebrews 10:24-25). It is my experience of watching people who have come to Christ that unless they meet together with other Christians, it is difficult for their faith to stay alive.

One man who found himself in this position was visited by a wise old Christian. They sat in front of the coal fire in the sitting room. The old man never spoke, but went to the coal fire and picked out a red-hot coal with some tongs and put it on the hearth. He still said nothing. In a few minutes the coal had lost its glow. Then he picked it up and put it back in the fire. After a short time it began to glow again. The old man still said nothing at all but, as he got up to leave, the other man knew exactly why he had lost his fervor—a Christian out of fellowship is like a coal out of the fire.

A young couple who had recently come to faith in Christ wrote:

> We have been coming to church for a year now and it already feels like home. The atmosphere of love, friendship, and excitement is impossible

> to find elsewhere. The joy of it far exceeds any evening at a pub, party, or restaurant . . . I am shocked to say (although I continue to enjoy all three!) Both of us find that Sunday's services and Wednesday's gatherings are two high points of the week. At times, it feels like coming up for air, especially as by Wednesday it is to be drowning in the deep waters of working life! If we miss either, we feel somehow "diluted." Of course, we can keep talking to God together and alone, but I feel that the act of meeting together is the bellows that keep on fanning the flames of our faith.

The body of Christ

Third, the church is the body of Christ. Paul had been persecuting the Christian church when he encountered Jesus Christ on the road to Damascus. Jesus said to him, "Saul, Saul, why do you persecute *me*?" (Acts 9:4, italics mine). Paul had never met Jesus before so he must have realized that Jesus was saying that, in persecuting Christians, he was persecuting Jesus Himself. It may well be that from his encounter Paul realized that the church was the body of Christ. "He calls the church Christ," wrote the sixteenth-century reformer, Calvin. We Christians are Christ to the world. As the old hymn says:

> He has no hands but our hands
> To do His work today;
> He has no feet but our feet
> To lead men in His way;
> He has no voice but our voice
> To tell men how He died;
> He has no help but our help
> To lead them to His side.

Paul develops this analogy in 1 Corinthians 12. The body is a unit (v. 12), yet this unity does not mean uniformity. Within the body there is almost infinite variety. People have different gifts and serve in different ways, but everybody fits in somewhere. God gives each of us a role in the church, not so we can show off, but for the common good (v. 7). If we don't play our part the whole body suffers. In this sense the church has been compared to a football game: twenty-two people desperately in need of a rest, being watched by twenty-two thousand people desperately in need of exercise. Each one of us represents Jesus and can do His good deeds wherever we go: in our families, at work, where we live, and with our friends.

John Wimber was once approached by a member of his congregation who had met somebody in great need. After the Sunday service this man told John Wimber of his frustration in trying to get help, "This man needed a place to stay, food, and support while he gets on his feet and looks for a job. I am really frustrated. I tried telephoning the church office, but no one could see me and they couldn't help me. I finally ended up having to let him stay with *me* for the week! Don't you think the church should take care of people like this?" John Wimber thought for a moment and then said, "It looks like *the church* did."

What should our attitude be to other parts of the body of Christ? Paul deals with two wrong attitudes.

First, he speaks to those who feel inferior and who feel that they have nothing to offer. For example, Paul says the foot may feel inferior to the hand or the ear inferior to the eye (vv. 14-19). It is a human tendency to feel envious of others.

It is easy to look round the church and feel inferior and therefore not needed. As a result we do nothing. In fact, we are all needed. God has given gifts "to each one" (v. 7). The term "to each one" runs through 1 Corinthians 12 as a common thread. Each person has at least one gift that is absolutely necessary for the proper functioning of the body. Unless each of us plays the part God has designed for us, the church will not be able to function as it should.

In the following verses, Paul turns to those who feel superior (vv. 21-25) and are saying to others, "I don't need you." Again, Paul points out the folly of this position. A body without a foot is not as effective as it might be (see v. 21). Often the parts that are unseen are even more important than those with a higher profile.

We need to recognize that we are all in it together; there is a mutual dependence, and each part affects the whole: "If one part suffers, every part suffers with it; if one part is honored, every part rejoices with it" (v. 26). When everybody is playing their part something really beautiful occurs, like an orchestra where many people are performing. Globally as well, this is true. Rather than dismissing other parts of the church because they are different from us, it is exciting to realize that we can be enriched by them.

A holy temple

Fourth, in the church we experience the presence of God. The only church building the New Testament speaks about is a building made of people. Paul says that the Christians are "being built together to become a dwelling in which God lives by his Spirit" (Ephesians 2:22). Jesus is the chief cornerstone. He is the one who founded the church and around whom the church is built. The foundations are "the apostles and prophets" and the result is a holy temple made of "living stones."

In the Old Testament the tabernacle (and later the temple) was central to Israel's worship. This was the place where people went to meet with God. At times His presence filled the temple (1 Kings 8:11) and especially the Holy of Holies. Access to His presence was strictly limited (see Hebrews 9).

Through His death on the cross for us, Jesus opened up access to the Father for all believers all the time. His presence is no longer confined to a physical temple; now He is present by His Spirit with all believers. His presence is especially sensed when Christians gather together (Matthew 18:20). His new temple is the church, which is "a dwelling in which God lives by his Spirit."

Professor Gordon Fee writes that presence "is a delicious word." If you love someone, what you want more than anything else is that person's presence. Letters are good; photos are great; telephone calls are fantastic. But what you really long for is their presence.[77] The presence of God was what Adam and Eve lost in the Garden of Eden. But God promised that He would restore His presence. First in the temple in the Old Testament and after Pentecost, when the Spirit of God was poured out, the presence of God came to live among His people.

Paul writes of individual Christians, "Do you not know that your bodies are temples of the Holy Spirit, who is in you, whom you have received from God?" (1 Corinthians 6:19). But more often he writes that the church, the gathered community of Christians, is the temple of the Holy Spirit. That is where God lives by His Spirit. Under the Old Covenant (before Jesus), access to the Father was through a priest

(Hebrews 4:14), who made sacrifices on behalf of believers. Now Jesus, our great high priest, has made the supreme sacrifice of His own life on our behalf. Jesus "appeared once for all at the end of the ages to do away with sin by the sacrifice of himself" (Hebrews 9:26). We do not need to make further sacrifices for our sins. Rather, we need to be constantly reminded of His sacrifice for us. At the service of Holy Communion, sometimes called the Lord's Supper or the Eucharist, we remember His sacrifice with thanksgiving and partake of its benefits.

As we receive the bread and wine we look in four directions:

We look back with thanks

The bread and wine remind us of the broken body and shed blood of Jesus Christ on the cross. As we receive Communion we look back to the cross with thankfulness that He died for us so that our sins could be forgiven and our guilt removed (Matthew 26:26-28).

We look forward with anticipation

Jesus could have left us some other way to remember His death, but He chose to leave us a meal. A meal is often a way in which we celebrate great occasions. One day in heaven we are going to celebrate for eternity at "the wedding supper" of Jesus Christ (Revelation 19:9). The bread and wine are a foretaste of this (Luke 22:16; 1 Corinthians 11:26).

We look around at the Christian family

Drinking from one cup and eating the one loaf symbolizes our unity in Christ. "Because there is one loaf, we, who are many, are one body, for we all partake of the one loaf" (1 Corinthians 10:17). That is why we do not receive the bread and the wine on our own. Eating and drinking together in this way should not only remind us of our unity, it should strengthen that unity as we look around at our brothers and sisters for whom Christ died.

We look up in expectation

The bread and wine represent the body and blood of Jesus. Jesus promised to be with us by His Spirit after His death, and especially wherever Christians meet together: "Where two or three come together in my name, there am I with them" (Matthew 18:20). So as we receive Communion we look up to Jesus with expectancy. In our experience, we have found that on such occasions there are sometimes conversions, healing, and powerful encounters with the presence of Christ.

The bride of Christ

Fifth, Jesus loves the church; it is the bride of Christ. This is one of the most beautiful analogies of the church in the New Testament. Paul says, when speaking of the husband and wife relationship: "This is a profound mystery—but I am talking about Christ and the church" (Ephesians 5:32).

To describe the relationship between God and human beings the New Testament uses analogies of the closest possible relationship. A prominent analogy, for example, is that of a parent to a child. Yet here Paul suggests that perhaps the best analogy is that of the love between a husband and a wife. That is the love that Jesus has for you. St. Augustine said, "God loves each one of us as if there was only one of us to love."

As the Old Testament speaks about God being a husband to Israel (Isaiah 54:1-8), so in the New Testament Paul speaks about Christ being a husband to the church and the model of every human marriage relationship. So he tells husbands to love their wives "just as Christ loved the church and gave himself up for her to make her holy, cleansing her by the washing with water through the word, and to present her to himself as a radiant church, without stain or wrinkle or any other blemish, but holy and blameless" (Ephesians 5:25-27).

This picture of the holy and radiant church may not entirely reflect its present condition, but we get a glimpse here of what Jesus intends for His church. One day Jesus will return in glory. In the Book of Revelation, John has a vision of the church, "the new Jerusalem, coming down out of heaven from God, prepared as a bride beautifully dressed for her husband" (Revelation 21:2). Today the church is small and weak. One day we shall see the church as Jesus intends it to be. In the meantime, we must try to bring our experiences as close as possible to the vision of the New Testament.

Our response to Christ's love for us should be one of love for

Him. The way we show our love for Him is by living in holiness and purity—being a bride fit for Him and fulfilling His purpose for us. This is His intention for us. This is how His purposes for us will be fulfilled. We are to be changed and to be made beautiful until we are fit to be His bride.

Jackie Pullinger, whom I have mentioned before, works particularly with heroin addicts and prostitutes in Hong Kong. Jackie met a seventy-two-year-old woman named Alfreda who had been a heroin addict and a prostitute for sixty years. When Jackie met her she used to sit outside a brothel all day in a run-down area of the city. She would inject heroin into her back three times a day, her legs and her arms having been overused. Without an identity card, as far as the Hong Kong government was concerned, she didn't even exist. She gave her life to Christ and she received forgiveness. She went to live in one of Jackie's houses and as God healed her she began to change.

Later, she met a man called Little Wa, who was seventy-five, and they got married. Jackie described their wedding as "the wedding of the decade" because Alfreda, a former prostitute and heroin addict, walked down the aisle in white, cleansed, forgiven, and transformed by the love of Jesus Christ. To me this is a picture of the church. There is only one way into the church, and that is to say, "God, be merciful to me, a sinner." When we say that, God in His love responds, "You are part of My people. You are My family. You are My representative; you are My body on earth. You are a holy temple; My Spirit lives within you. You are My bride."

CHAPTER 15

HOW CAN I MAKE THE MOST OF THE REST OF MY LIFE?

We only get one life. We might wish for more. D. H. Lawrence said, "If only one could have two lives. The first in which to make one's mistakes . . . and the second in which to profit by them."[78] But there are no dress rehearsals for life; we find ourselves on stage immediately.

Even if we have made mistakes in the past, it is possible with God's help to make something of the future. How can we make the most of the rest of our lives? Paul tells us in Romans 12:1-2 how we can do this:

> Therefore, I urge you, brothers, in view of God's mercy, to offer your bodies as living sacrifices, holy and pleasing to God—this is your spiritual act of worship. Do not conform any longer to the pattern of this world, but be transformed by the renewing of your mind. Then you will be able to test and approve what God's will is—his good, pleasing and perfect will.

What should we do?

Break with the past

As Christians, we are called to be different from the world around us. Paul writes, "Do not conform any longer to the pattern of this world" (by which he means the world that has shut God out). Or as J. B. Phillips translates this verse, "Don't let the world around you squeeze you into its own mold." This is not easy; there is a pressure to conform. It is very hard to be different.

A young police officer was taking his final exam at Hendon Police College in north London. Here is one of the questions:

> You are on patrol in outer London when an explosion occurs in a gas main in a nearby street. On investigation you find that a large hole has been blown in the footpath and there is an overturned van lying nearby. Inside the van there is a strong smell of alcohol. Both occupants—a man and a woman—are injured. You recognize the woman as the wife of your Divisional Inspector, who is at present away in the U.S. A passing motorist stops to offer you assistance and you realize that he is a man who is wanted for armed robbery. Suddenly a man runs out of a nearby house, shouting that his wife is expecting a baby and that the shock of the explosion has made the birth imminent. Another man is crying for help, having been blown into an adjacent canal by the explosion, and he cannot swim.
>
> Bearing in mind the provisions of the Mental Health Act, describe in a few words what actions you would take.

The officer thought for a moment, picked up his pen, and wrote, "I would take off my uniform and mingle with the crowd."

We can sympathize with his answer. As a Christian, it is often easier to take off the uniform and "mingle with the crowd." But we are called to remain distinctive, to retain our Christian identity, wherever we are and whatever the circumstances.

A Christian is called to be a chrysalis rather than a chameleon. A chrysalis is a pupa which turns into a beautiful butterfly. A chameleon is a lizard with the power to change color: many can assume shades of green, yellow, cream, or dark brown. It is thought to change color to match its background. Similarly, chameleon Christians merge with their surroundings, happy to be Christians in the company of other Christians, but willing to change their standards in an environment that is not Christian. Legend has it that an experiment was carried out on a chameleon. It was put on a tartan background, could not take the tension, and exploded! Chameleon Christians experience an almost unbearable tension in their lives and, unlike chrysalis Christians, do not reach their full potential.

Christians are not called to fit in with their backgrounds, but to be different. Being different does not mean being odd. We don't have to start wearing weird clothes or speaking in a peculiar religious language. We can be normal! A friendship with God through Jesus Christ should help each of us to become fully human—all that God intended us to be. In this sense, the more like Jesus we become, the more normal we become. When the nineteenth century philosopher Søren Kierkegaard became a Christian, he declared, "Now, with God's help, I will become myself."[79]

When we follow Christ, we are free to shed patterns and habits that bring us and others down. For example, it means that we should no longer indulge in character assassination behind people's backs.

It means that we do not need to spend our time grumbling and complaining (if that is what we were like before). It also means that we are free not to conform to the world's standards of sexual morality. This might all sound very negative, but in fact, the opposite is the case. Rather than being backbiters, we should be encouragers, constantly looking to build others up out of love for them. Rather than grumbling and complaining, we should be full of thankfulness and joy. Rather than indulging in sexual immorality, we should be demonstrating the blessing of keeping God's standards.

This latter example is one area where Christians are called to be different, but which many find difficult. In my experience of speaking about the Christian faith there is one subject which arises time and time again—the whole question of sexual morality. Questions most frequently asked in this area are, "What about sex outside marriage? Is it wrong? Where does it say so in the Bible? Why is it wrong?"

God's pattern here, as elsewhere, is so much better than any other. God invented marriage. He also invented sex. He is not, as some seem to think, looking down in astonishment and saying, "Oh my goodness, whatever will they think of next?" C. S. Lewis pointed out that pleasure is God's idea, not the devil's. The Bible affirms our sexuality and it celebrates sexual intimacy: in the Song of Songs we see the delight, enjoyment, and satisfaction it brings.

The inventor of sex also tells us how it can be enjoyed to the full. The biblical context of sexual intercourse is the lifelong commitment in marriage between one man and one woman. The Christian doctrine is set out in Genesis 2:24 and quoted by Jesus in Mark 10:7, "For this reason a man will leave his father and mother and be united to his wife, and the two will become one flesh." Marriage involves the public act of leaving parents and making a lifelong commitment. It involves being "united" with one's partner—the Hebrew word meaning literally "glued" together—not just physically and biologically, but emotionally, psychologically, spiritually, and socially. This is the Christian context of the "one flesh" union. It is God's plan that children should be brought up in a context of love, and therefore commitment. The biblical doctrine of marriage is the most exciting, thrilling, and positive view of marriage that exists, and arguably the most romantic. It sets before us God's perfect plan.

God warns of the danger of going outside the boundaries He has laid down, of ignoring the instructions. There is no such thing as "casual sex." Every act of sexual intercourse effects a "one flesh" union (1 Corinthians 6:13-20). When this union is broken people get hurt. If you glue two pieces of cardboard together and then pull them apart, you can hear the sound of ripping and see that bits of each are left behind on the other. Similarly, becoming one flesh and then being torn apart leaves scars. We leave broken bits of ourselves in broken relationships. All around us we see what happens when God's standards are ignored. We see broken marriages, broken hearts, hurt children, sexual disease, and those whose lives are in a mess. On the other hand, in so many Christian marriages where God's standards are kept, we see the blessing that God intended to bestow on the whole area of sex and marriage.

Of course, it is never too late. God's love through Jesus can bring forgiveness, heal scars, and restore wholeness to lives that have been torn apart. Jesus wants to restore wholeness to our lives and to give us a new start.

So, let us not allow the world to squeeze us into its mold. Let us show the world something far, far better.

Make a new start

Paul says we are to "be transformed" (Romans 12:2). In other words, we are to be like the chrysalis which changes into a beautiful butterfly. Many are fearful of change in their life: two caterpillars sitting on a leaf saw a butterfly passing by. One turned to the other and said, "You won't catch me going up in one of those!" Such is our fear of leaving behind what we know.

God does not ask us to leave behind anything that is good. But He does ask us to get rid of the rubbish. Until we leave the rubbish behind we cannot enjoy the wonderful things God has for us. There was a woman who lived on the streets and walked round our parish. She would ask for money and react aggressively to those who refused. She walked the streets for years, accompanied by a mass of plastic bags. When she died, I presided over the funeral. Although I didn't expect anyone to be there, there were in fact several well-dressed people at the service. I discovered afterwards that this woman had inherited a large fortune. She had acquired a luxurious flat and many valuable paintings, but she chose to live on the streets with her plastic bags full of rubbish. She could not bring herself to leave her lifestyle, and she never enjoyed her inheritance.

As Christians we have inherited far more—all the riches of Christ. In order to enjoy these treasures, we have to leave behind the rubbish in our lives. Paul tells us to "hate what is evil" (v. 9). That is what must be left behind.

In the verses that follow (Romans 12:9-21) we get a glimpse of some of those treasures to be enjoyed:

> Love must be sincere. Hate what is evil; cling to what is good. Be devoted to one another in brotherly love. Honor one another above yourselves. Never be lacking in zeal, but keep your spiritual fervor, serving the Lord. Be joyful in hope, patient in affliction, faithful in prayer. Share with God's people who are in need. Practice hospitality. Bless those who persecute you; bless and do not curse. Rejoice with those who rejoice; mourn with those who mourn. Live in harmony with one another. Do not be proud, but be willing to associate with people of low position. Do not be conceited.

Do not repay anyone evil for evil. Be careful to do what is right in the eyes of everybody. If it is possible, as far as it depends on you, live at peace with everyone. Do not take revenge, my friends, but leave room for God's wrath, for it is written: "It is mine to avenge; I will repay," says the Lord. On the contrary: "If your enemy is hungry, feed him; if he is thirsty, give him something to drink. In doing this, you will heap burning coals on his head." Do not overcome by evil; but overcome evil with good.

Sincere love

The Greek word for "sincere" means "without hypocrisy," or literally "without play acting" or "without a mask." Often, relationships in the world are quite superficial. We all put up fronts to protect ourselves. When we see governments doing this, we call it "spin." When we do it ourselves, we call it "image;" we are projecting something. I certainly did this before I was a Christian (and it carried on to some extent afterwards—though it shouldn't have). I said, in effect, "I don't really like what I am inside, so I will pretend I am somebody different."

If other people are doing the same then there are two "fronts" or "masks" meeting. The real people never meet. This is the opposite of "sincere love." Sincere love means taking off our masks and daring to reveal who we are. When we know that God loves us as we are, we are set free to take off our masks. This means that there is a completely new depth and authenticity in our relationships.

Enthusiasm for God

Sometimes people are cynical about enthusiasm, but there is nothing wrong with it. There is a joy and excitement, a "spiritual fervor" (v. 11) that comes from our relationship with God. This initial experience of Christ is meant to last, and not to peter out.

Some people have an amazing initial experience of Christ. Some will not feel anything, and some will experience great difficulties. However, what really matters is where they are in their relationship with God in ten years' time. Similar to a marriage, it's the long term that is of the most importance. It doesn't matter whether or not you have a great honeymoon. Some do, some don't. I know of one couple who got so sunburned that they couldn't touch each other for the whole two weeks! I met someone recently who told me that their grandparents went on a barge for their honeymoon. On the first night, the barge sank; they had to bail themselves out and then get a bus home! But sixty-three years later they're very happily married; that's what matters. Paul says, "Never be lacking in zeal," but, "keep your spiritual fervor, serving the Lord." The longer we have been Christians, the more enthusiastic we should be.

Harmonious relationships

Paul urges Christians to live in harmony with one another and to be generous (v. 13), hospitable (v. 13), forgiving (v. 14), empathetic (v. 15), and to live at peace with everyone (v. 18). It is a glorious picture of the Christian family into which God calls us, beckoning us into an atmosphere of love, joy, patience, faithfulness, generosity, hospitality, blessing, rejoicing, harmony, humility, and peace, where good is not overcome by evil, but evil is overcome by good. These are some of the treasures in store when we leave behind the rubbish.

How do we do it?

"Present your bodies ..."

This requires an act of the will. Paul commands us, in view of everything that God has done for us, to offer our bodies as living sacrifices, holy and pleasing to God (Romans 12:1). God wants us to offer all of ourselves and all of our lives.

First, we offer our time. Our time is our most valuable possession and we need to give God all of it. This does not mean we spend all of it in prayer and Bible study, but that we allow His priorities to be established in our lives. It is easy to get our priorities wrong. An advertisement appeared in a newspaper: "Farmer seeks lady with tractor with view to companionship and possible marriage. Please send picture—of tractor."

One of the things that happens when we give everything to God is that people become much more important than possessions. Our priorities must be our relationships, and our number one priority is our relationship with God. Starting the day by reading the Bible and praying always has an impact on the rest of the day. We need to set aside time to be alone with Him. We also need to set aside time to be with other Christians—on Sundays and perhaps at some mid-week meeting where we can encourage one another.

Second, we need to offer our ambitions to God, saying to Him, "Lord, I trust you with my ambitions and hand them over to you." He asks us to seek His kingdom and His righteousness as our foremost ambition and then He promises to meet all our other needs (Matthew 6:33). This does not necessarily mean that our former ambitions disappear; they may become secondary to Christ's ambitions for us. There is nothing wrong with wanting to be successful in our job, provided that our motivation in everything is seeking His kingdom and His righteousness, and that we use what we have for His glory.

Third, we need to offer Him our possessions and our money. In the New Testament there is no ban on private property, making money, saving, or even enjoying the good things of life. What is forbidden is a selfish accumulation for ourselves, an unhealthy obsession with material things, and putting our trust in riches. What promises security leads to perpetual insecurity and leads us away from God (Matthew 6:19-24). Generous giving is the appropriate response to the generosity of God and the needs of others around us. It is also the best way to break the hold of materialism in our lives.

Next, we need to give Him our ears—do we listen to gossip or do we attune our ears to hearing what God is saying to us through the Bible, through prayer, through books, and talks and so on? We offer Him our eyes and what we see. Again, some things we look at can harm us through jealousy, lust, or some other sin. Other things can lead us closer to God. Rather than criticizing the people we meet, we should see them through God's eyes and ask, "How can I be a blessing to that person?"

Then we need to give Him our mouths. The apostle James reminds us what a powerful instrument the tongue is (James 3:1-12). How many people can look back to something said to them at school or by a parent that has had a negative influence on their whole life? Do we use our tongues to deceive, curse, gossip, draw attention to ourselves, or to speak well of others?

Further, we offer Him our hands. Do we use our hands in violence or to take for ourselves? Or do we use them to give and to serve?

Finally, we offer Him our sexuality. Do we use it for our own gratification or do we reserve it for the good and pleasure of our marriage partner?

We cannot pick and choose. Paul says, "Present your bodies"—that is every part of us. The extraordinary paradox is that as we give Him everything, we find freedom. Living for ourselves is slavery; but "His service is perfect freedom" (as the *Book of Common Prayer* puts it).

"... as living sacrifices"

There will be a cost to doing all this. It may involve some sacrifice. As the commentator William Barclay put it, "Jesus came not to make life easy but to make men great."[80] We have to be prepared to go God's way and not ours. We have to be willing to give up anything in our lives which we know is wrong and put things right where restitution is required, and we need to be willing to fly His flag in a world that may be hostile to the Christian faith.

In many parts of the world, being a Christian involves physical persecution. More Christians died for their faith in the twentieth century than in any other. Others are imprisoned and tortured. We, in the free world, are privileged to live in a society where Christians are not persecuted. The criticism and mocking we may receive are hardly worth mentioning compared to the suffering of the early church and the persecuted church today.

Nevertheless, our faith may involve making sacrifices. For example, I have a friend who was disinherited by his parents when he became a Christian. I know one couple who had to sell their home because they felt that as Christians they must let the Inland Revenue know that over the years they had not been entirely honest in their tax returns.

I had a great friend who was sleeping with his girlfriend before he became a Christian. When he began to look at the Christian faith, he realized that this would have to change if he put his faith in Christ. For many months he wrestled with it. Eventually both he and his girlfriend became Christians and decided that from that moment they would stop sleeping together. For various reasons they were not in a position to get married for another two-and-a half years. There was a sacrifice involved for them, although they do not see it in that way. God has blessed them richly with a happy marriage and four wonderful children. But at the time there was a cost involved.

Why should we do it?

What God has planned for our future

God loves us and wants the very best for our lives. He wants us to entrust our lives to Him so that we can "test and approve what God's will is—his good, pleasing and perfect will" (Romans 12:2).

I sometimes think that the chief work of the devil is to give people a false view of God. The Hebrew word for "Satan" means "slanderer." He slanders God, telling us that He is not to be trusted. He tells us God is a spoilsport and that He wants to ruin our lives. Often we believe these lies. We think that if we trust our Father in heaven with our lives He will take away all our enjoyment in life. Imagine a human parent like that. Suppose one of my sons were to come to me and say, "Daddy, I want to give you my day to spend it however you want." Of course, I would not say, "Right, that is what I have been waiting for. You can spend the day locked in the cupboard!"

It is absurd even to consider that God would treat us worse than a human parent. He loves us more than any human parent and wants the very best for our lives. His will for us is *good*. He wants the very best (as every good parent does). It is *pleasing*— it will please Him and us in the long run. It is *perfect*—we will not be able to improve on it.

However, sadly it's true that people often feel they *can* improve on it. They think, "God is a bit out of touch. He hasn't caught up with the modern world and the things that we enjoy. I think I will run my own life and keep God well out of it." But we can never do a better job than God, and sometimes we end up making an awful mess.

One of my sons was given some homework that involved making an advertisement for a Roman slave market. It was a school project and he spent most of the weekend doing it. When he had finished the drawing and written all the inscriptions, he wanted to make it look 2,000 years old. The way to do that, he had been told, is to hold the paper over a flame until it goes brown, which gives it the appearance of age. It is quite a tricky job for a nine-year-old, so my wife Pippa offered to help—several times—but could not persuade him. He insisted on doing it himself. The result was that the advertisement was burned to a cinder, accompanied by many tears of frustration and hurt pride.

Some people do not want any help, they will not trust God, and often it ends in tears. But God gives us a second chance. My son did his poster again and this time he trusted Pippa to do the delicate singeing operation. If we will trust God with our lives, then He will show us what His will is—His good, pleasing, and perfect will.

What God has done for us

The little sacrifices He asks us to make are nothing when we compare them with the sacrifice that God made for us. C. T. Studd, the nineteenth-century England cricket captain who gave up wealth and comfort (and cricket!) to serve God in inland China, once said, "If Jesus Christ be God, and he died for me, nothing is too hard for me to do for him."[81] The writer of Hebrews urges us, "Let us run with perseverance the race that is set before us, looking to Jesus the pioneer and perfecter of our faith, who for the joy that was set before him endured the cross, despising the shame, and is seated at the right hand of the throne of God" (Hebrews 12:1-2, RSV).

As we look at Jesus, God's only Son, who "endured the cross," we see how much God loves us. It is absurd not to trust Him. If God loves us so much we can be sure He will not deprive us of anything good. Paul wrote, "He who did not spare his own Son, but gave him up for us all—how will he not also, along with him, graciously give us all things?" (Romans 8:32). Our motivation for living the Christian life is the love of the Father. Our model in life is the example of the Son. The means by which we can live this life is the power of the Holy Spirit.

How great God is and what a privilege it is to be in a relationship with Him, to be loved by Him and to serve Him all our lives. It is the best, most rewarding, fulfilling, meaningful, satisfying way to live. Indeed, it is here we find the answers to the great questions of life.

ENDNOTES

1. Ronald Brown (ed.), *Bishop's Brew* (Arthur James Ltd., 1989).
2. Barack Obama, *The Audacity of Hope: Thoughts on Reclaiming the American Dream* (Canongate Books Ltd., 2008), p. 202.
3. By kind permission of Bernard Levin.
4. *Ibid.*
5. Leo Tolstoy, *A Confession and Other Religious Writings* (Penguin, 1988).
6. C. S. Lewis, "Timeless at Heart" in *Christian Apologetics* (Fount, 2000).
7. Francis Collins, *The Language of God* (Free Press, 2006).
8. Alexander Solzhenitsyn, *The Gulag Archipelago, 1918-1956: An Experiment in Literary Investigation - Volume One* (Basic Books, 1997).
9. Quoted by Philip Yancey, *What's So Amazing about Grace* (Zondervan, 1997), p. 279.
10. *The Sunday Times*, September 22, 2001.
11. Paul Tillich, *Writings on Religion*, ed. Robert P. Scharlemann (Walter de Gruyter, 1987), p. 160.
12. Josephus, *Antiquities*, XVIII 63f. Even if, as some suggest, the text has been corrupted, nonetheless the evidence of Josephus confirms the historical existence of Jesus.
13. F. F. Bruce, *The New Testament Documents: Are They Reliable?* intro. N. T. Wright (Eerdmans, 2003), p. 11.
14. F. J. A. Hort, *The New Testament in the Original Greek*, Vol. I (Macmillan, 1956), p. 561.
15. Sir Frederic Kenyon, *The Bible and Archaeology* (Harper and Row, 1940).
16. If you are interested in pursuing the subject of gospel historicity, I would recommend reading N. T. Wright, *Jesus and Victory of God* (SPCK, 1996) or Craig Blomberg, *The Historical Reliability of the Gospels* (IVP Academic, 2007).

17. C. S. Lewis, *Mere Christianity* (Fount, 1952).
18. *Ibid.*
19. Bernard Ramm, *Protestant Christian Evidences* (Moody Press, 1971).
20. By kind permission of Bernard Levin.
21. A team of medical experts produced a detailed study of the physical effects of the treatment which Jesus' body was made to endure based on such circumstantial details and concluded that as a result of hypovolemic shock and exhaustion asphyxia, it would have been a medical impossibility for Jesus to have been alive when he was taken down from the cross (there is a report of the study in *Journal of the American Medical Association*, Vol. 255, March 21, 1986).
22. Josh McDowell, *The Resurrection Factor* (Here's Life Publishers, 1981).
23. Michael Green, *Man Alive* (Inter Varsity Press, 1968).
24. Sir Arthur Conan Doyle, *The Sign of Four* (Penguin, 2001).
25. C. S. Lewis, *Mere Christianity* (Fount, 1952).
26. Raniero Cantalamessa, *Life in Christ* (Vineyard Publishing, 1997) p. 7.
27. Jeffrey Myers, *Somerset Maugham* (University of Michigan Press, 2004), p. 347.
28. Bishop J. C. Ryle, *Expository Thoughts on The Gospel*, Vol. III, John 1:1-John 10:30 (Evangelical Press, 1977).
29. John Stott, *The Cross of Christ* (Inter Varsity Press, 1996). See also *Catechism of the Catholic Church*, Chapter 2, line 444, paragraph 615, entitled: "Jesus substitutes his obedience for our disobedience." By his obedience unto death, Jesus accomplished the substitution of the suffering Servant, who "makes himself an *offering for sin*," when "he bore the sin of many," and who "shall make many to be accounted righteous," for "he shall bear their iniquities."
30. Raniero Cantalamessa, *Life in Christ* (Vineyard Publishing, 1997) pp. 52-3.
31. We deal with religious concepts using metaphors and parables. For the atonement there is no one seminal metaphor, no one all-encompassing parable. All are approximations, which like the

radii of a circle, converge on the same central point without ever quite touching it.

32. John Wimber, *Equipping the Saints* Vol. 2, No. 2, Spring 1988 (Vineyard Ministries, 1988).
33. Lesslie Newbigin, *Foolishness to the Greeks* (SPCK, 1986), p. 127.
34. C. S. Lewis, *The Last Battle* (HarperCollins, 1956).
35. Andrew Murray, *Believer's Secret of the Master's Indwelling* (Bethany House Publishing, 1986).
36. C. S. Lewis, *Weight of Glory* (HarperOne, 2001).
37. For further reading on this subject I recommend Pete Greig, *God on Mute* (Kingsway, 2007).
38. See John Micklethwait and Adrian Wooldridge, *God is Back: How the Global Rise of Faith is Changing the World* (Allen Lane, 2009), p. 177 and p. 266.
39. Stanley Baldwin, *This Torch of Freedom* (Ayer Publishing, 1971), p. 92.
40. Quoted in Alister McGrath's Commemorative Lecture to the Latimer Trust, 2005.
41. For further reading on this subject, please see Nicky Gumbel, *Searching Issues* (Kingsway, 2002) and *Is God a Delusion?* (Alpha International, 2008).
42. Albert Einstein, *Ideas and Opinions* (Crown Publishers, Inc., 1954).
43. John W. Wenham, *Christ and the Bible* (Tyndale: USA, 1972).
44. *Dei Verbum*, Chapter 3, 11.
45. John Pollock, *Billy Graham: the Authorised Biography* (Hodder & Stoughton, 1966).
46. Bishop Stephen Neill, *The Supremacy of Jesus* (Hodder & Stoughton, 1984).
47. Rick Warren, *The Purpose-Driven Life* (Zondervan, 2002) p. 186.
48. To help start reading the Bible, please see: Nicky Gumbel, *30 Days* (Alpha International, 1999) or other Bible reading notes.
49. Philip Yancey and Paul Brand, *In the Likeness of God* (Zondervan, 2004) p. 218.
50. J. I. Packer, *Knowing God* (Hodder & Stoughton, 1973).
51. Michael Bordeaux, *Risen Indeed* (Darton, Longman & Todd, 1983).
52. Oscar Wilde, *The Importance of Being Earnest and Other Plays* ed. Richard Allen Cave (London, Penguin Classics, 2000) p. 147.

53. The slightly old-fashioned sense of the word 'ghost' in this context shares a root with the German word *geist*, which means "spirit" (as in "zeitgeist").
54. This is my adaptation of the account as narrated by Charles Marsh in *The Beloved Community: How Faith Shapes Social Justice from the Civil Rights Movement to Today* (New York: Basic Books, 2005).
55. Corrie ten Boom and Jamie Buckingham, *Tramp for the Lord* (CLC, 1974), p. 55.
56. F. W. Bourne, *Billy Bray: The King's Son* (Epworth Press, 1937).
57. Pope John Paul II, *You Have Received a Spirit of Sonship* (Vatican City, 1993).
58. J. Hopkins and H. Richardson (eds.), *Anselm of Canterbury, Proslogion Vol I* (SCM Press, 1974).
59. Malcom Muggeridge, *Conversion* (Collins, 1988).
60. Richard Wurmbrand, *In God's Underground* (Hodder & Stoughton, 1977).
61. Discourses III.13
62. Jürgen Moltmann, *The Church in the Power of the Spirit* (Fortress Press, 1993), p. 297.
63. Murray Watts, *Rolling in the Aisles* (Monarch Publications, 1987).
64. There has been a great deal of discussion in recent years about whether this experience of the Holy Spirit should be described as "baptism," "filling," "releasing," "empowering" or some other term. What is clear is that we need the experience of the power of the Holy Spirit in our lives. I myself think that the filling of the Holy Spirit is the most faithful to the New Testament and I have used that expression in this chapter.
65. Martyn Lloyd-Jones, *Romans*, Vol. VIII (Banner of Truth, 1974).
66. Saint Augustine, *The Confessions*, trans. R. S. Pine-Coffin (Penguin Classics, 1961), p. 21.
67. John Wimber and Kevin Springer (eds), *Riding the Third Wave* (Marshall Pickering, 1987).
68. Alan MacDonald, *Films in Close Up* (Frameworks, 1991).
69. Michael Green, *I Believe in Satan's Downfall* (Hodder & Stoughton, 1981).
70. C. S. Lewis, *The Screwtape Letters* (Fount, 1942).

71. C. S. Lewis, *The Great Divorce* (Fontana, 1974), p. 113.
72. The two terms are synonymous. "Heaven" was a common Jewish expression for referring to God without mentioning the divine name. The Jewish background to Matthew's Gospel, as opposed to the Gentile orientation of Luke and Mark, probably explains the different use.
73. Raniero Cantalamessa, *Come Creator Spirit* (The Liturgical Press, 2003), p. 277.
74. Some years ago Dr. Rex Gardner, a Fellow of the Royal College of Obstetricians and Gynecologists, investigated a series of cases of alleged healing miracles. His conclusions were as follows: "Intellectual honesty demands that (after discounting cases with dubious diagnoses, those where psychosomatic considerations are important, and others where the cure might be attributable to adjuvant medical therapy or where spontaneous remission might be the explanation) there remain some cures for which medicine has no explanation…[I]n these cases the constant association of prayer to God cannot be discounted. Nor can it be set aside as merely a psychological 'boost', for some of the healings cannot have a psychosomatic explanation…[I]n absolute terms the number [of miraculous healings] appears to be fairly rapidly increasing as more churches become open to this work of God; and percentage-wise more are being healed as the Holy Spirit is being permitted to develop ministries within local fellowships." R. F. R. Gardner, *Healing Miracles: A Doctor Investigates* (Darton, Longman and Todd, 1986), p. 205-206.
75. The degree and location of Christian persecution around the world is continually changing. For more information and details on how to support and pray for this part of the church see, for example, www.opendoorsuk.org
76. David Watson, *I Believe in the Church* (Hodder & Stoughton, 1978).
77. Gordon Fee, *Paul, The Spirit and the People of God* (Hodder & Stoughton, 1997).
78. James T. Boulton (ed.), *The Selected Letters of D. H. Lawrence* (Cambridge: Cambridge University Press, 2000), p. 396.

79. Søren Kierkegaard, *Papers and Journals*, ed. Alastair Hannay (Penguin Classics, 1996), p. 295.
80. William Barclay, *The Parables of Jesus* (Westminster John Knox Press, 1999), p. 221.
81. Norman P. Grubb, *C. T. Studd, Cricketer and Pioneer* (CLC, 1985), p. 141.

the alpha store

what do we need to run an alpha course?

QUESTIONS OF LIFE-REVISED

The Alpha course talks in book form. Containing the 15 talks, this is essential reading for anyone involved in leading an Alpha course. This book is also available in individual chapter booklets. 105021

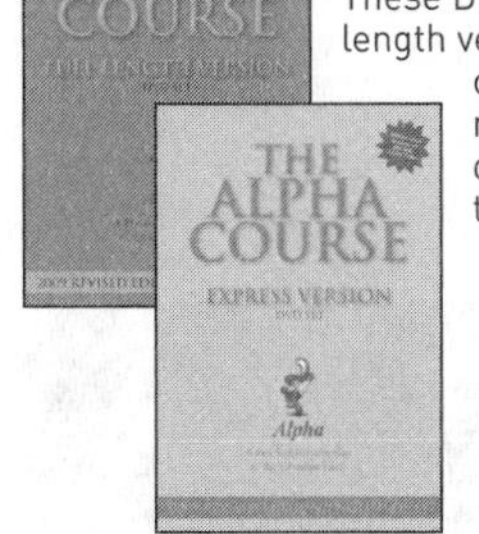

THE ALPHA COURSE DVD FULL LENGTH AND EXPRESS VERSIONS

These DVD sets comprise the 15 talks for the Alpha course. The full length version includes the complete talks, whereas the express version contains talks that have been shortened to between 20-25 minutes in length. *Alpha Express* is ideal for use in the workplace or in other contexts where there may be less than an hour to run the course. 15153 / 15154

THE ALPHA COURSE CLASSIC GUEST MANUAL

The "classic" guest manual that everyone loves, has been refreshed on the outside with a bold new color and a revised interior, while preserving all the wonderful illustrations by Charlie Mackesy. This provides a guide through the talks and key points. It provides lots of white space for free-form notes, thoughts, and questions. 15205

THE ALPHA COURSE GUEST MANUAL

This newly designed manual is a "must have" for all guests on the Alpha course, as well as for hosts and helpers. This essential resource is now even more appealing for guests and its new design makes it easier to use. The manual contains newly revised content and has a fresh and contemporary feel. 15204

30 DAYS

An excellent introduction to Bible reading designed to be read over thirty days. Nicky Gumbel has selected thirty passages from the Old and New Testaments which he has found particularly helpful. It is designed to complement the talk "Why and How Should I Read the Bible?" on the Alpha course and is also ideal for others who are interested in beginning to explore the Bible. 54057

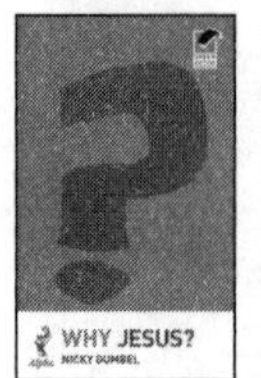

WHY JESUS?

An evangelistic booklet for those having their first thoughts about the Christian faith. It is designed to be given to all guests at an Alpha dinner, during the course, or at church services or events. 20072

WHY CHRISTMAS?

A Christmas version of *Why Jesus?* 20081

WHY EASTER?

An Easter version of *Why Jesus?* 20075

what do we need to train the team?

THE DIRECTOR'S HANDBOOK

An invaluable guide covering the administrative needs for every stage of setting up and running an Alpha course. Includes reusable checklists, forms for recording and organizing information, guidance on setting up the Weekend Away, guest services, and celebration dinners. 17150

HOW TO RUN THE ALPHA COURSE DVD

In this DVD Nicky Gumbel provides the essential foundation for anyone thinking of setting up an Alpha course. It includes talks on the principles and practicalities of Alpha as well as a talk on Integrating Alpha into the local church. Presented at an Alpha Conference. Filmed in 2001. 17152

THE ALPHA COURSE TEAM TRAINING DVD

These three training sessions should be given to all hosts and helpers prior to running each Alpha course. Contains sessions and common questions and answers on:

- Leading Small Groups [61 mins]
- Pastoral Care [62 mins]
- Ministry on Alpha [57 mins]

Includes a humorous sketch on "How Not to Host a Small Group". 25606

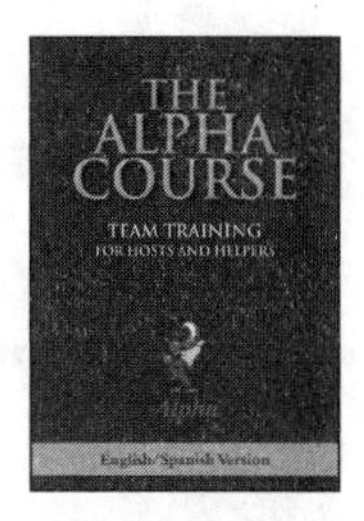

THE ALPHA COURSE TEAM TRAINING GUIDE

For all hosts and helpers on the Alpha course—the guide provides notes on the hosts' training material and includes practical reminders, suggested discussion prompts, and key Bible verses for each week. Essential for every Alpha small group host and helper. 15389

SEARCHING ISSUES

Nicky Gumbel tackles the seven most common objections to the Christian faith, including suffering, other religions, and sex before marriage. Recommended reading for all course leaders and small group hosts prior to an Alpha course. This book is also available in individual chapter booklets. 105023

what do we need to introduce alpha to our church?

JUST CURIOUS KIT

For anyone interested in running an Alpha course or presenting the idea to others. Includes 1 of each of the following: *Questions of Life book; The Alpha Course Manual; How to Run the Alpha Course: Telling Others* book; *Why Jesus?* booklet; *Alpha Course Introductory* DVD, *What Is Alpha* promotional brochure and a copy of *Alpha News*. 83378

ALPHA COURSE INTRODUCTORY DVD

This new promotional DVD will help churches see how valuable the Alpha model is in linking churches with like passion. Includes the Alpha Invitation; What is Alpha?; Alpha Stories; the 60 sec. high impact commercial; "Is There More to Life Than This?" sample talk by Nicky Gumbel and some advertising help from Bear Grylls. 80977

WHAT IS ALPHA? BOOKLET FOR PASTORS AND GUESTS

A giveaway informational brochure with testimonies, quotes, and endorsements about Alpha. One unique for pastors and leaders and an new one for handing out to prospective guests. Perfect for anyone with questions about the course. 80979 / 80980

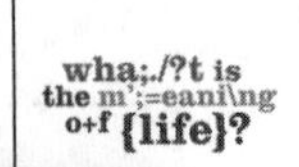

THE GOD WHO CHANGES LIVES SERIES

Collections of fantastic faith-building stories of people whose lives have been dramatically touched by God. Vol 1 100648 / Vol 2 100649 / Vol 3 100650 / Vol 4 100652 / The American Collection 100651

what do we need for follow-up after alpha?

A LIFE WORTH LIVING

This nine-week Bible study is based on Paul's letter to the Philippians and examines the changed life of a Christian. Nicky Gumbel offers practical and encouraging insights for living the Christian life, while covering such topics as having a new heart, finding a new purpose, and gaining a new confidence. 105024

JESUS LIFESTYLE SERIES 1, 2, AND 3

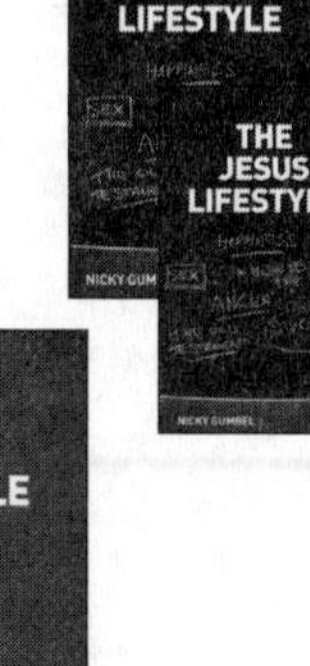

This study examines Jesus' teaching in the Sermon on the Mount and the radical alternative that it presents to the modern lifestyle. Eighteen sessions in 3 6-session DVD series with manuals for each series. For both mature and new believers, this practical study addresses such topics as how to have an influence on society, how to handle money, and how to get our relationships right.

Series 1 DVD 25321 manual 25322
Series 2 DVD 25323 manual 25324
Series 3 DVD 25325 manual 25326
The Jesus Lifestyle: text book to the course 25327

If you are interested in finding out more about Alpha please contact:

Alpha U.S.A.
2275 Half Day Road
Suite 185
Deerfield, IL 60015
Tel: 800.362.5742
Tel: + 212.406.5269
e-mail: info@alphausa.org
www.alphausa.org

Alpha Canada
Suite #230 – 11331 Coppersmith Way
Riverside Business Park
Richmond, BC V7A 5J9
Tel: 800.743.0899
Fax: 604.271.6124
e-mail: office@alphacanada.org
www.alphacanada.org

Alpha in the Caribbean
Holy Trinity Brompton
Brompton Road
London SW7 1JA UK
Tel: +44 (0) 845.644.7544
e-mail: americas@alpha.org
www.alpha.org

To purchase resources in Canada:

David C. Cook Distribution Canada
P.O. Box 98, 55 Woodslee Avenue
Paris, ON N3L 3E5
Tel: 800.263.2664
Fax: 800.461.8575
e-mail: custserve@davidccook.ca
www.davidccook.ca

online
alpharesources.org
alpha.org

phone
800.362.5742
212.406.5269

email
info@alphausa.org
office@alphacanada.org